The Socially Constructed
Organization

Other titles in the
Systemic Thinking and Practice Series
edited by David Campbell & Ros Draper
published and distributed by Karnac Books

Credit Card orders, Tel: 020-7584-3303; Fax: 020-7823-7743;
Email: books@karnacbooks.com

The Socially Constructed Organization

David Campbell

Foreword by
John Shotter

Systemic Thinking and Practice Series
Work with Organizations

Series Editors
David Campbell & Ros Draper

London & New York
KARNAC BOOKS

First published in 2000 by
H. Karnac (Books) Ltd., 58 Gloucester Road, London SW7 4QY

A subsidiary of Other Press LLC, New York

British Library Cataloguing in Publication Data

A C.I.P. for this book is available from the British Library

ISBN 1 85575 034 0

10 9 8 7 6 5 4 3 2 1

Edited, designed, and produced by Communication Crafts

Printed in Great Britain by Polestar AUP Aberdeen Limited

www.karnacbooks.com

CONTENTS

This book represents a significant development of the concept that underpins the Systemic Thinking and Practice Series. For a number of years, the ideas of social constructionism have been interweaving with those of systemic thinking, and many practitioners use concepts and techniques from both fields with equal facility. However, in this book the author has distinguished the different fields very clearly, while discussing the links between them. He has expanded this series by moving systemic thinking closer to one of its neighbouring fields of thought.

An alternative title for this book might be "Social Constructionism in Action", for the author has taken the ideas of constructionism from the philosophy seminar into the world of organizational consulting. He has put them to work in many challenging situations across a wide range of organizations, which he describes with many first-hand examples. It is a personal book because the author describes, in detail, how he works with various types of organizations. His idiosyncrasies mingle with his efforts to frame his work within a social constructionist model, and the reader certainly does learn how he works.

The book will be of interest to anyone who works in organizations. Although the author writes about his consultation work, the book is also rich in discussion about what makes organizations tick. There are, for example, many suggestions about initiating "essential conversations" within an organization whether one is in the position of an employee or in that of an external consultant.

David Campbell
Ros Draper
London
June 2000

FOREWORD

John Shotter

It used to be thought that when we talked of organizations and of organizational behaviour, there was something
already there of a definite character to be talked about. David
Campbell, however, takes a quite different social constructionist
stance in this book towards organizations and organizational
behaviour. It is a stance that works in terms of "the relatedness
of everything around us". Thus, as he sees it, an organization is
something that "is being constructed continuously on a daily, even
momentary, basis through individual interactions with others.
The organization never settles into an entity or a thing that can be
labelled and described, because it is constantly changing, or reinventing itself, through the interactions going on within it". It is
a dynamically changing setting for its members' actions, just as
when driving down a multi-lane motorway we all must react and
respond to how we are placed at any one moment in relation to all
the others around us. In other words, strangely, whether we are
workers within "it" or consultants from outside "it", we do not
exactly know what we are talking about when we claim to be
talking about "an organization". Yet, it does a have certain charac-

ter to it, such that, like driving on the motorway, not just anything goes. "It" is something we have to get a sense of.

We need a set of methods for socially constructing between us—those of us within "it" and those of us outside—yet further features, refinements, or elaborations of something fluid and still developing. This is David Campbell's achievement in this book.

As he remarks in the Introduction (in a way that, to my mind, is rather unnecessarily apologetic), the ideas he presents are not meant to represent the world. Indeed not. For the task is not to give an accurate picture of what already exists, but to bring into existence what does not yet exist—a new facet or feature of a practice that suddenly makes (socially constructs) a connection or link between things that could have been connected, but were not.

In the past, when researchers thought that of necessity they had to be scientific, it is as if they came on the scene too late and looked in the wrong direction. They looked back as intellectually trained individuals, in terms of a special research tradition, to discover supposedly already existing hidden centres of influence (to which their tradition was especially oriented), claiming that these gave people's behaviour in an organization its structure. But now, what David Campbell wants to do is to come on the scene much earlier, to treat everyone involved as operating prior to the time of them receiving any special training in one or another intellectual discipline. We are all treated much more as just ordinary, everyday people. Indeed, in an unapologetic fashion, he declares that he has written this book "resolutely for practitioners". And central to it is conversational talk: it is the consultant's task not to solve an organization's problems for it, but to create a number of safe conversational forums within an organization such that those within it can come to create the new relations between themselves that are necessary for new ways forward.

This emphasis on face-to-face conversational talk is why Campbell emphasizes the use of metaphors and gives working examples. For, in teaching a practice, it is precisely these two moves that are important. This is because, along with a relatedness, we must also put an emphasis on people being spontaneously responsive to each other—this is where the inherent creativity of dialogue comes in. When someone says, "Look at it this way", and then gives a new metaphor for what is going on in the organization, others find themselves responding to it in new ways, in ways that suggest new connections between things not previously noticed.

Examples too are very important in this way. Wittgenstein (1969) is well known for remarking that "not only rules, but also examples are needed for establishing a practice. Our practice leaves loop-holes, and the practice has to speak for itself" (p. 139). Thus it is that we find that talk of "striking" examples helps in establishing a new practice. They "tell" us a new way of responding, and, in so doing, they establish new ways of seeing, new forms of perception for use in making sense of all the other "things" we encounter in the practice. Hence Campbell's extensive use of examples in this book. Principles need interpreting; they arouse unending intellectual debate.

The final proof of this book, says Campbell, will be in "whether the ideas and examples are presented in a way that is perceived as trustworthy, persuasive, and, ultimately, useful". And he has achieved it marvellously well. But this is not just Campbell's task, the consultant's task, but, as any good manager in an organization knows—as we all in our everyday lives know—it is the task we all face in attempting to get the others around us to coordinate their actions with ours in achieving something worthwhile. This book will be a resource for all those inside and outside organizations to draw on.

Introduction

> Apparently, Samoans engage in what is called a *maaloo exchange*. For example, if I have done something well and you commend me for it, the *maaloo exchange* requires that I respond by recognising your essential assistance in my successful performance. In other workers the *other-as-supporter* is central to Samoan understanding. For instance . . . after a group of travellers return from a trip and are greeted with a welcome home, the exchange might be: "Well done the trip", to which the returning travellers respond: "Well done the staying back."
>
> E. Sampson, 1993, p. 68

Social constructionism is a growing field of study. It is also a very loosely assembled body of knowledge, which makes it easier for theorists and writers to select one or two components and carry them away to define and develop their own versions of social constructionism. I have found this both stimulating and frustrating. It is difficult to pull the diverse strands into one coherent framework, but on the other hand the field invites creative application of the ideas. However, there has been very little systematic application of social constructionist ideas to work done with organizations. This lack is what this book is about.

This is a field of study and practice I can contribute to. For several years I have been using social constructionist ideas, both as an employee and a staff member in several places of work and as a consultant to various small organizations in the private and public sector. This book is an opportunity to gather my experiences together and reflect on the ways social constructionist ideas have helped (or, in some cases, not) organizations to overcome obstacles and move forward.

Think of this book as a metaphor. It contains ideas that are not meant to represent the world but may nevertheless help you, the reader, survive in your own organization or make effective interventions as a consultant to other organizations. I like the metaphor of a toolbox, with each of these ideas being used to help tackle a particular problem, but my female colleagues have said: "How typical of a man to choose the metaphor of the toolbox!" One of them offered instead the metaphor of a chest with many drawers, each one containing ideas for a different purpose. I hope you will choose your own metaphor.

Writing this book has helped me to identify what is compelling, for me, about organizations—the potential for continuous interaction with others that allows me to "take a stand" in many small ways throughout the day and to have others respond to me, giving me feedback about where I stand or who I am. At the same time, living within an organization allows me to "lose myself" in something much larger, more powerful, and more mysterious than my own life.

I grew up in a family that had strong opinions, and since I was the last child, I felt that the family values were not open for negotiation by the time I came along. It was as though one had to accept them "lock, stock, and barrel", or find some other means of expressing one's voice. So I am today fascinated by the way realities are created and held in place through a social process, and how an individual can take part in the process without losing his or her own voice. For me, social constructionism is a metaphor that helps me take another step forward.

Part I of the book presents the ideas I have selected and fitted together as my own version of social constructionism. I have amalgamated the ideas of many people in the field to create a framework for understanding a bit more about how organizations work.

Part II reflects my attempts to put the social constructionist framework to work. I want to quash any illusions that this is an advanced or fully conceptualized enterprise. I am on the lower rungs of this ladder, but I have taken the time over the past several years to think differently about my work with organizations. I am in the process now of trying to develop new techniques of construction that are consistent with the theoretical framework.

Several years ago I read a quotation from one of the balloonists who had attempted to circumnavigate the globe. After a ditched attempt, he said: "I don't think we have failed—we have just found another way that didn't work." With this attitude of learning from experience, I am presenting in Part III two extended case illustrations—one that appeared to have a good outcome and one that did not—which the reader might like to try to generalize from to his or her own work setting. I hope that the reader will appreciate from these consultations the experimental nature of the book—the attitude that "we will simply have to try certain things and wait to see how the organization responds".

The book ends with some final thoughts on social constructionism and work with organizations.

For those readers who are familiar with social constructionist concepts, you may be more interested to read how some of the work has been done, and I suggest you begin at Part II, which is based on real case examples, and then perhaps return to Part I for a review of the conceptual framework. (I have tried reading the book in this way, and it does seem to work.)

I have written this book, resolutely, for practitioners. I am not trying to develop the various intellectual debates in the field, of which there are many, but rather to touch on the relevant concepts and theoretical arguments that will enhance the practice of living within or working with organizations. The final proof of the book, for me, is whether the ideas and examples are presented in a way that is trustworthy, persuasive, and, ultimately, useful.

A CONCEPTUAL FRAMEWORK

CHAPTER ONE

Social constructionism and systemic thinking

Systemic thinking is a way to make sense of the relatedness of everything around us. In its broadest application, it is a way of thinking that gives practitioners the tools to observe the connectedness of people, things, and ideas: everything connected to everything else. Certainly, people from all walks of life—from the mystic to the medical practitioner, from the ecologist to the engineer—are "thinking systemically" when they address the interconnectedness within their field of vision, but within the social sciences, and particularly the field of family therapy, the discourse about the relatedness of people has been heavily influenced by *general systems theory* (von Bertalanffy, 1950; see also Ashby, 1956)

This body of theory has been advanced and applied to the social sciences over the past 30 years by such people as Anderson, Goolishian, and Winderman (1986), Bateson (1972), Boscolo, Cecchin, Hoffman, and Penn (1986), Hoffman (1981, 1993), Keeney (1983), and Von Foerster (1981), and readers should turn to these sources for a fuller unfolding of systemic thinking. General systems theory has given us all a language to organize the world in

7

certain ways. Advocates speak about *differences* which constitute the mutual *feedback* that connects people and reveals a *pattern* of behaviour. They speak of behaviour acquiring *meaning* from the *context* in which it is observed by an active *observer* of one *part* of the larger system which represents the *whole*. And these tools have been applied to many different clinical and organizational settings, to such an extent that there is now a rich body of knowledge, or a discourse, that generates clinical practice, research methodologies, and, of course, dialogue amongst its adherents. Many of these concepts were developed in the field of family therapy, where practitioners found that thinking of the family as a system was a metaphor indispensable for their work.

However, most people in this field acknowledge that during the early 1980s a paradigm shift was taking place from traditional general systems theory, known as "first-order cybernetics", towards "second-order cybernetics" which placed the observer firmly within the system that he or she was observing. The emphasis shifted towards the constructs that the observer brought with him or her as the observation of a family began and, then, towards the reciprocal influence that the observer and the family had upon each other. Rather than viewing a system as something connected by feedback and difference, the emphasis shifted towards the system as a meaning-generating entity. The reciprocal activity between the observer and the family resulted, in some mysterious way, in creating new meanings for all those who participated in the process. The way was opened for new models or metaphors that would shed some light on the mystery of collaborative meaning-making.

Social constructionism emerged from a different academic tradition and poses different types of questions. Its roots lie in the field of sociology and, in particular, George Mead's "symbolic interactionism" (1934a), which offered the view that we construct our own identities through interaction with others. However, Berger and Luckmann's *The Social Construction of Reality* (1966) is usually cited as the seminal text that launched this new field. They described a social process whereby ideas are placed in the public domain and then become "true" as they are taken up in various forms of public debate and turned into "objective facts".

The philosophical tradition of post-structuralism (Saussure, 1974) led various thinkers to reconsider the modernist view of a truth "out there" waiting to be discovered, and literary critics such as Bakhtin (1993) suggested that the meaning of literary texts did not reside in the intention of the author or the embedded structures of the text itself, but, rather, in the way that the reader constructed his or her own meaning from within his or her own temporal and cultural context.

From the field of psychology, Kenneth Gergen (1985) and Rom Harré (Harré, 1979) have explored the concepts of self and identity. Gergen proposes that we are not one "self" but construct different "selves" to create "voices" to influence relationships around us. Different voices are required in different contexts, and it is these voices that are the basis of our sense of self. Harré takes this thinking one step further by saying that our sense of identity results from the way beliefs about our self are conveyed to us through language. He would argue, for example, that the language of Western societies is dominated by the logic of individuals making active choices in their environment, which contributes to the notion that we must then have "selves" capable of autonomous activity.

Whereas the central concern of systems thinking has been identifying the patterns that connect different parts of a larger system, social constructionism has always asked *how* people work together to produce the realities that we all live by. It distinguishes itself from systemic thinking by moving from the question of "what is happening" to the question of "how does it happen", or from the "observation of pattern" to the "explanation of action".

I am sure that many readers will have their own explanation of the evolution of social constructionism as a parallel trajectory to systems thinking, but my own version is that systemic thinking was adopted as the predominant metaphor for many therapists, because one of its pioneers—the anthropologist and biologist Gregory Bateson—was invited to join a research project in the 1960s with a group of family therapists interested in the origins of schizophrenia. They developed models of pathological communication in families, culminating in 1956 in the double-bind theory. These concepts were highly influential in the fledgling field of family therapy. However, had one of the followers of Mead's symbolic interactionists, perhaps a sociologist, been invited to join this group, the course of development might have been very different!

But, in the end, both systems theory and social constructionism are metaphors that enable us to function in a particular context. Whereas the metaphor of systems thinking helped us make sense of interconnectedness and ecology, perhaps the metaphor of social constructionism facilitates an understanding of the way realities are construed from the voices of many people from many parts of the world. This book explores the possibility that this metaphor will also help us understand our relationship to organizations. What follows is a discussion of the specific conceptual tools that I have found useful in creating my own social constructionist model for work with organizations.

De-construction before construction

The critics and philosophers who de-constructed literary criticism challenged a basic assumption that meaning was inherent in the structures of literary texts, and they suggested instead that each reader should create his or her own meaning within a specific cultural context. The "meaning" of a Jane Austen or Henry James novel today is to be found in the interpretations made by the readers, from certain cultural backgrounds and at the present time. Edward Said (1994) has discussed the cultural biases that Western Europeans or Americans bring to their interpretation of non-Western literature.

The legacy of this literary debate has been the licence to review the assumptions underlying some cherished concepts in contemporary social sciences. Erica Burman (1994) in her book *Deconstructing Developmental Psychology* has examined the cultural influences that lead us to make certain assumptions about how children develop, and Phoenix, Woollett, and Lloyd (1991) have applied the same critical lens to the process of motherhood.

What all of this suggests is that it is not possible to study the way realities are constructed without first examining the underlying assumptions—the basic paradigm—that the participants bring with them to the process. It is clear that the basic tools for our thinking are rooted in certain paradigms and belief systems, such as scientism, Cartesian duality, formal logic, or systemic pattern; if we accept these tools without challenge, we will never be able to think beyond the paradigm itself.

This is highly relevant for organizational life. Organizations, as we shall see, certainly create their own belief systems, and then people within them find it a struggle to discover new solutions within the old paradigm. A culture for de-constructing basic assumptions may be essential as a first step.

Knowledge is constructed between us

The central premise of social constructionism is that knowledge is constructed between us. The traditional view that the world exists "out there", and that we use our brains, logic, and language to discover the truth of the world, is being supplanted by the idea that the realities we observe are created by mutual influence with other people. For example, within an organization individuals have their own views, and when they begin to interact with others they inevitably constrain or influence others towards some ways of thinking and feeling and away from other ways of thinking and feeling. Over time, the mutually constraining process produces a "house paradigm" that all have come to believe, because they have no other.

The philosopher Richard Rorty makes this point beautifully by quoting a passage about poetry from Harold Bloom's *Kabbalah and Criticism*:

> The sad truth is that poems *don't have* presence, unity, form or meaning . . . What then does a poem possess or create? Alas, a poem *has* nothing and *creates* nothing. Its presence is a promise, part of the substance of things hoped for, the evidence of things not seen. Its unity is in the good will of the reader . . . its meaning is just that there is, or rather *was*, another poem. [in Rorty, 1989, p. 122]

"Let us give up the failed enterprise of seeking to "understand" any single poem as an entity in itself. Let us pursue
instead the quest of learning to read any poem as its poet's
deliberate misinterpretation, *as a poet* of a precursor poem or of
poetry in general. [p. 43]

I understand this to suggest that a poem is an attempt to de-
construct a small part of the world we know. A poet deliberately
challenges accepted interpretations, challenges understanding, and
sets the reader on another course.

Language as a social process

One of the central assumptions underpinning social constructionism is about language. Social constructionists distinguish a pre-
Wittgenstein concept of language as a medium to connect us to the
real world from the Wittgensteinian definition of language as a set
of tools that enables us to build realities as we describe them
(Wittgenstein, 1953).

The former definition of language suggests that there is a world
of thoughts, feelings, and objects "out there" which is separate
from a "mind", in our possession, that observes, describes, and
makes sense of the world out there. Language is the medium that
connects the self to reality and allows us to carry out this operation. Language, through grammar and vocabulary, may or may
not be sufficient for the task of accurate description. This view
leads to questions such as: "Does my description fit the world?" or
"Am I being faithful to the true nature of the self?" Rorty, who has
helpfully evaluated these ideas, says that these assumptions will
naturally follow "once we accept the idea there are non-linguistic
things called 'meanings' which it is the task of language to express,
as well as the idea that there are non-linguistic things called 'facts'
which it is the task of language to represent" (1989, p. 13).

An alternative view of language has been presented by
Kenneth Gergen (1994) as a central platform of social constructionism. This is that the function of language is not to represent reality
but to enable us to engage in social relations, and the meanings

that we construe about the world result from these social inter-actions. He draws on Wittgenstein's argument that words acquire their meaning "through the ways they are used in patterns of ongoing exchange" (Gergen, 1994, p. 52).

Gergen also refers to Austin's (1962) definition of the performative aspect of language, which emphasizes, not whether it corresponds with fact, but whether language fits into a social act and helps to coordinate the actions of the people involved in the act. Gergen is leading towards the position that language helps us to maintain relationships with "communities of understanding", such as employees within an organization, and it is these communities that will define the realities they want to adhere to.

Metaphor

The social constructionist view of language is a pragmatic one. Some words or ideas are more successful in helping us to cope with life. I am reminded of the story of the airline pilot who is more successful with the concept "the earth is round", whereas the architect designing a tennis court is more successful with the concept "the earth is flat". Language is judged on the basis of its usefulness in helping people coordinate their thoughts and actions within various communities, such as families, readers of books, players of games, and, of course, work colleagues.

Other writers have described the evolutionary view of language—that is, new words and concepts killing off the old to adapt to a changing environment. Rorty (1989) makes the point that if you take the view that language is a medium, you might say that Galileo made a discovery—"he finally came up with the words which were needed to fit the world properly" (p. 19)—whereas one who sees language as pragmatic and evolutionary might say that he hit upon a tool that happened to work better for certain purposes than any previous tool. "Once we found out what could be done with a Galilean vocabulary, nobody was much interested in doing the things which could be done with an Aristotelian vocabulary" (p. 19).

Rorty goes on to discuss ideas about metaphor, and as a consultant interested in change I have found these very helpful. He begins by making a distinction between the literal and metaphorical, not in terms of two sorts of meaning but as a distinction between the familiar and the unfamiliar. Metaphors are unfamiliar; they have not yet been absorbed into "meaningful" language. Metaphors do not have meanings; rather, they are tossed into a conversation—the equivalent of making a face or pulling a photograph out of your pocket. These are ways of producing an effect on your conversation partner, but they are not ways of conveying a specific message. It is not appropriate to respond to a metaphor by asking: "What exactly are you trying to say?"

> If one had wanted to say something—if one had wanted to utter a sentence with a meaning—one would presumably have done so. But instead one thought one's aim could be better carried out by other means. . . . An attempt to state that meaning would be an attempt to find some familiar (that is, literal) use of words—some sentence which already had a place in the language game. [p. 18]

Fitting into the familiar is also constraining the participants to only certain meanings that have already been agreed upon, whereas the metaphor may be used in conversation to introduce a difference to the conventional meaning of the words being used.

Certain metaphors will catch on, others will not. Think of DNA originating as a metaphor, which offered new tools to the scientific community and has now become part of the language game—that is, it has specific meaning and can be proven to be literally true or literally false, until a new metaphor arrives to lead science to new understanding within the gene project. The problem with the literally true or false sentence, according to Rorty, is that it becomes a "dead metaphor" which allows us to accept certain truths about our conversations and to stop searching for new meanings: "The literal uses of sentences are the uses we can handle by our old theories about what people will say under various conditions. Their metaphorical use is the sort which makes us get busy developing a new theory" (p. 17).

What is the relevance of metaphors for the social constructionist view of organizations? If we can appreciate that we organize much of our thinking about organizations in metaphorical concepts such as "cooperation requires compromise" or "time is a resource", we become aware that this is not a "truth" but a metaphorical construction that highlights certain properties or relations while suppressing others. We can appreciate that metaphors reflect cultural values, and therefore we can look outside the organization towards the wider social discourse to understand some of the ideas that drive the organization. And, finally, we can appreciate that because metaphors allow us to "do certain things better than others", we can evaluate metaphors for their capacity to help us do things. If they are not helpful, they can be jettisoned for new metaphors that stand up to the test of pragmatic usefulness.

The meaning of the "self"

"If the body had been easier to understand, nobody would have thought that we had a mind."

R. Rorty, 1980

For some time, social constructionists have argued that, in Western societies, we all operate with a mistaken notion of what an "individual" is and how we develop a sense of self (see Mills, 1940). These are complex philosophical arguments, for which readers may want to refer to other sources, but several of them can be spelt out here. Sampson (1993), for example, criticizes the Western emphasis on the individual as an economic unit, with his or her own thoughts and the ability to act in an autonomous fashion. Sampson argues that, on the contrary, we learn who we are in relation to others, and we act as the result of many influences from the environment around us, many of which we are not aware of.

Shotter (1989) offers a fascinating account of the way language encourages us to develop a sense of the self which is bounded by our own skin. The use of the pronoun "I" encourages us to locate one's own self somewhere inside, "as something unique and distinct from all else that there is", and it is the existence of this "self" that guarantees one's personal identity. The "I" becomes the source of all thought, meaning, and language. The self becomes the "knower", "distinct from what there is to be known, able to gain knowledge from the world in an individual and autonomous way" (p. 137), which locks us into a hermetic Cartesian dualism. But compare this with the pronoun "me", which is experienced as an object that we can possess like any other. "Me-ness" is equivalent to other attributes or qualities such as intelligence, height, or freckles. If "me" is somehow external, then it also belongs to other worlds. It can have originated from other sources and can be connected to other external experiences.

Shotter elaborates by referring to the work of Benveniste, who claims that "I" does not have a consistent reality in the way the noun "chair" does, but is made up and defined in a unique way each time it is used: "What then is the reality to which I and you refer? It is solely a 'reality of discourse' and this is a strange thing. I cannot be defined except in terms of 'location'. I can only be identified by the instance of discourse in which it [the I] is produced" (Benveniste, 1971, p. 218).

The "self" created by others

> "From our beginning as children, and continuing on into our lives as adults, we are dependent upon being addressed by others for whatever form of autonomy we may achieve."
>
> Shotter, 1993, p. 143

Our sense of who we are depends upon what meaning others make of us and how they convey that meaning back to us. This is an essential premise that underpins all of social constructionist thinking: the sense of who one is, the self, the I, are all constructed in the interaction between the individual and others. "People owe what stability and constancy and uniqueness and identity they may appear to have" (Shotter, 1993) to the practices and activities that enable them to make their differences known and recognized by other people. In other words, the constancy in our lives is not a reflection of an inner self that repeats its actions and beliefs over and over, but, rather, a function of being in consistent, supportive, and respectful relationships that enable individuals to receive consistent messages from others.

Contemporary social constructionists emphasize this process as a life-long and continuous function of communication. Because we each need an audience to confirm the meaning of what we say and do, much of the aim of language is to preserve an audience and to gather from it the responses we need to maintain an evolving sense of identity. This places us not in an ontological context of "being who we are", but in a moral and pragmatic context of saying and doing the necessary things to maintain dialogue with an appropriate audience. Shotter says:

> I act not simply "out of" my own plans and desires . . . but also in some sense "in to" the opportunities offered me to act. . . . And my action in being thus "situated" takes on an ethical or moral quality. I cannot just relate myself to others around me as I myself please: the relationship is ours, not just mine, and in performing within it I must proceed with the expectation that you will intervene in some way if I go "wrong". [p. 144]

We have now travelled a long way from the idea that language is a medium to connect the self to reality. Social constructionists take the view that we use language to coordinate the relationship between ourselves and our audience and, through the coordination, to arrive at a meaning for what we are doing and what is going on around us. The coordination seems to work something like this: in social settings we are continually negotiating with others about how to position ourselves, or "how to be", in order that others will acknowledge us, attribute meaning to our behaviour, and make us accountable for who we are and how we are behaving.

We are continually attempting to mean something to someone else. And if we are communicating in order to create a meaning-making relationship with others, we must pay attention to how others might respond to us. Again in Shotter's terms, "an understanding of how they might respond is part of our understanding of who they are for us" (1993, p. 145) or what they mean for us, and we hope that they will have similar thoughts of what we mean to them.

Mills makes the powerful point that "rather than expressing something which is prior and in the person, language is taken by other persons as an indicator of future actions" (in Shotter, 1993, p.

141). For me, these ideas have clarified two important issues for organizational life. The first is that employees are doing several things when they communicate with each other, one of which is trying to clarify what they should do next within the conversation but also within the organization as a whole. The other issue is that when they are communicating, they are involved in a mutual meaning-making process. In my experience, the time spent addressing these issues in working with organizations has been time well spent, as I discuss later.

Discourse

In order to place this meaning-making activity in a wider social context that is appropriate to organizations, we need to review the concept of discourse. This is defined by Burr (1995) as "a set of meanings, metaphors, representations, images, stories, statements and so on that in some way produce a particular version of events". Since each conversation creates its own version of events, there is a limitless number of metaphors and larger social discourses that can be created to represent an event or a thing, like an organization, to the world. For example, Morgan (1986), in his influential *Images of Organisations*, essentially spells out eight possible discourses that can be used to represent organizations, using labels such as "the organization as a political system", a "machine", a "brain". Within each discourse, there are theories, practices, structures, and operations that cohere to give some meaning to the behaviour of the people working within the organization, and these are expressed in company reports, notice-boards, employment practices, as well as the conversations around the water-coolers.

Burr also highlights the recursive, two-way process between discourses and the things that people actually say or write about— that is, discourses can be revealed in the things people say, but these things are dependent for their meaning on the discursive context in which they appear. The social constructionist view is that the organization is not made up of individuals, each with their own attitudes or opinions that they bring to the conversation to influence others; rather, the things people say are thought of as "instances of discourse" or "occasions where particular discourses are given the opportunity to construct an event in this way rather than that" (Burr, 1995, p. 50). This is a crucial point because, as each organization creates discourses about itself, this enables us to see more clearly the organizational influence on individual behaviour.

Let us take, for example, two discourses that "appear" in most agencies I have observed: the *discourse of hierarchy* and the *discourse of shared responsibility*. A discourse of hierarchy might represent the agency as a structured organization, with some people at higher levels making decisions and passing them down to those working at lower levels. Within this discourse, some information should only be available to a few people, employees should do what they are asked by those above them, and different responsibilities should be reflected in different rates of pay. Standing around the water-cooler, the employees drawing on this discourse might be expected to say things like: "My manager is not giving me clear guidelines about my work", or "We need a special group of senior people to sort out this problem".

A different discourse within the same agency might represent it to the world as a place where everyone is consulted before important decisions are made, "but it means we have to share the responsibility if things don't work out". This discourse would aim to represent the agency in a different way by drawing attention to different aspects and working practices and, most importantly, by creating different implications for how people should behave in the agency. Conversations drawn from this discourse might sound like: "No one has a clear vision of where this organization is going" or "Why don't we meet to prepare some proposals for the others to consider?"

Opportunities and constraints

Within the framework of organizational discourse, certain ideas and actions are possible whereas others are constrained. One can see from the previous examples that a "discourse of hierarchy" will encourage, make possible, or afford only certain ways of thinking and acting, and while employees are acting within the opportunities offered by that discourse, any alternative actions that are associated with the "discourse of shared responsibility" are not made possible.

There is one great advantage in moving away from the view that organizational behaviour is motivated by individual attitudes and beliefs, and towards this view of organizational discourse. It enables us to see more clearly the operations at work that influence our behaviour on a daily basis, and it gives us the tools to change these operations if we choose so to do. Organizational behaviour can be seen as an attempt by individuals to create meaning with other people and then to position oneself within a wider discourse in the organization. This process can be brought into the light of day. But we still need some conceptual tools that allow us to understand how discourses are created, how they influence behaviour, and how they can be de-constructed.

The individual in social discourse

I want to suggest that each of us is motivated by the desire to take part in meaning-constructing relationships with others, and part of this process is being recognized for what we feel we are "really experiencing" and then having this validated through the ability to influence people and events from our own point of view. In other words, we can only be sure that we are acknowledged for what we are if we observe the effects of our "having influence" upon relationships around us. I have argued above that each conversation that takes place in an organizational context is an attempt to have the meaning of our words acknowledged through dialogue; on a larger scale, I think that people choose certain aspects of the discourses available to them to have some power and influence to control events around them.

For example, if one powerful discourse in an organization is about providing the best possible service to clients *regardless* of pay and working conditions, it will be difficult for an individual to be recognized as having a different view (such as an urgent need for improved pay and working conditions) if he or she can only be influential within that particular discourse. To speak within the discourse may compromise the individual who wants to say something very different, whereas to speak outside the discourse may afford that person less power to influence the organization. This seems to me a very helpful idea: that individuals in organizations often have to compromise between positioning themselves within parts of the discourse which allow them to express what they are experiencing, on the one hand; and parts of the discourse which afford them power and influence, on the other.

Gergen (1989) has explored these ideas with his concept of "warranting voice". He suggests that we present representations of ourselves that are most likely to "warrant voice", or to give our own version of events some validity and legitimacy. Those people in organizations whose voices prevail are those with authority and power; those in powerful positions "warrant voice" more easily than others. But organizations will have many voices competing for influence, and the people who "warrant voice" are also those who can "use the discourses" most effectively—that is, to speak their own mind within the powerful discourses of the organization or to initiate new ideas from within the discourse of the old.

Position

Another central idea in social constructionism is the concept of position. Think for a moment about the relationship we may have with a parent or child or partner. It is multifaceted in that there are many concepts of partner in our minds: the partner at home, at work, in the kitchen, in the bedroom, with children, with his or her parents, happy, angry, exercising, eating, and so on. Each of these versions of a partner is the result of a series of events that are brought together in our minds to make a meaningful pattern. The partner participates in many relationships and groups that offer her or him certain positions that she or he can take in that particular context. For example, the child of a farming family or of alcoholic parents is offered a finite number of positions to take within the relationships and the discourse in that community.

If we move from the concept of self towards the concept of position, it gives us the ability to see people occupying many different positions in many different discourses. This leads to a view that dialogue is not between selves taking the "I" position, but between two people in different positions within a larger discourse who are able to shift positions as they are influenced by the other's position in the dialogue process.

Power

"Being unable to fortify justice, we have justified force."

Blaise Pascal, *Pensées*

To understand the way discourses and individuals within them compete for power and influence, many social constructionists have turned to the writings of the French philosopher Michel Foucault (1972). His great contribution to the field is his historical analysis of the way society has controlled its citizens through the creation of institutions such as medicine, law, and education, each with its own ideology about how people should behave in society. These institutions define normal behaviour by creating expertise, or what Foucault calls "knowledge", which brings power with it. Power is not a quality that some people possess and others do not, but, rather, it is the ability to draw on certain discourses, or bodies of knowledge, to define the world in a way that allows you to do the things you want.

He describes a dynamic relationship among different discourses in society such that any prevailing discourse—such as "This organization should be driven by clear policies"—is continually subjected to critique and challenge from other competing discourses. Power and resistance are two sides of the same coin. Any prevailing or "dominant" discourse has power only in relation to other discourses that present alternative views. It is as though the power of the dominant discourse is seen in the relative weakness of alternative discourses. Only when the dominant discourse ceases to be "in dialogue" with alternative discourses can power no longer be exercised and force then used to get what one wants.

Burr (1995) emphasizes this point in the following way:

> You could say if it were not for this resistance, there would be no need to re-affirm constantly the truthfulness of these discourses. For example, if the notion that "a woman's place is in the home" were really secure in its position as a prevailing truth *or dominant discourse* there would be no need to keep asserting it. [p. 71, emphasis added]

Foucault does not believe that dominant discourses are "thought up" by powerful people, but, rather, that the social and cultural conditions of our lives give rise to certain ways of representing the world and all of us. Then, once a discourse is available, it becomes appropriated by people with power and influence in our society: writers, journalists, scientists, politicians, captains of industry, and so forth. By attempting to understand the social and cultural events that give rise to new discourses, or what he calls the "archaeology of knowledge", and the way they are turned into dominant discourses through the exercise of power, he hopes to be able to challenge the legitimacy of particular dominant discourses and to illuminate the "marginalized" discourses that have not been so powerfully represented.

The implications of these ideas for organizational life are enormous. For example, I have found it very helpful to think of the organization as a political arena in which dominant discourses organize daily activity in an environment in which the alternatives have become devalued and marginalized. It can be very helpful to discuss with an organization the reasons why a dominant discourse has come into being—and remains in place—and it can be equally helpful to discuss the alternative discourses that are crucial to keep dominant discourses in place. (This process is discussed further in part II.) This difficulty in stepping outside the dominant discourse is one of the greatest obstacles to organizational change.

Time

Another process that makes change difficult in organizations is that we may begin to see the dominant discourse as universal and timeless. As creatures of habit and pattern, we avoid chaos by giving meaning to the patterns we see around us, which means that we are likely to fit today's experiences into yesterday's explanation—for the ease of "getting on with life". Yet if we can create a version of Foucault's "archaeology of knowledge" to define a discourse as suitable for a *particular context* and at a *particular time*, it will mean that new discourses will be needed for the new context that arises with the passage of time.

Time also calibrates the process of change in a non-blaming fashion. So often I find that people have become attached to particular discourses, and then the political struggle to change the dominant discourse becomes personal and gets laden with much extra baggage from the past. On the other hand, if evolving discourses are seen as products of the passage of time, it becomes easier for people to let go and assume that new discourses will be required, regardless of the power struggles involved. This is the first step in bringing everybody on board the process of change.

The dialogic

"Moving closer and closer apart . . ."

A. D. Hope, poet

Bakhtin (1986) cautions that understanding and empathy can become a kind of fusion that suppresses dialogic communication and creates another platform for monologic communication. True dialogue cannot occur if one party is defined by the standpoint of another. Defining the other is a common means of establishing power and dominance over another person or group, and therefore dialogue only happens when each party is coming to the conversation free of control by the other. Any dominant group will lose its advantage in a true dialogue.

Much of my own work with organizations centres around trying to create dialogue, and I use many of these ideas as my starting point. For example, the employees in any agency must believe and see that the organization is fair, and they must also be aware of what they might lose as well as gain by opening up a dialogue. Finally, I try to create an interest in what might be learned about themselves or their departments, and what might be learned about others, through a dialogic conversation. I am continually trying to prepare an environment in which people will allow themselves to be influenced by others.

Hermens and Kempen (1993) have done some interesting research into the dialogic process. They propose that a dialogue is not a two-stage process but a three-stage process: "In the first step, A might say: 'this is my view.' In the second step, B responds: 'I have another way of seeing it.' In the third step, A changes more or less his or her initial view: 'Now I look at it in another way'" (p. 158). Hermens and Kempen were able to support this view with a research study that demonstrated the way subjects had changed initial assumptions in ways that were directly influenced by the values put forth by his or her partner in dialogic exchanges.

The other

"The 'otherness' which enters into us makes us other."

G. Steiner, 1989, p. 188

Perhaps the most powerful critique of the Western Enlightenment idea of a unified, authentic self is the ethical and moral one. Many writers have turned their attention to the process by which our sense of identity, our sense of self, rests on our relationship with the non-self or the "other" (Kitzinger & Wilkinson, 1996). To be a man, we must experience women as the "other"; to be white, we must experience black as the "other". But, as Sampson (1993) asserts, "it is wrong to assume that self and other are always equal contributors to the co-constructive process. Some have more power to set the terms of co-construction than others" (p. 143), and he continues: "the point is simple: if I *find myself* in and through you, but no longer control the you that grants me my self, then I am forced to deal with a self that is beyond my control, and I may not always enjoy this self with which I must now contend" (p. 155).

* * *

"What the devil are they up to?"

C. Geertz, 1979

Some writers, such as Geertz (1979) and Bakhtin (1981), warn that suppression of true dialogue happens when one partner in a dialogue is seeking fusion into "one-ness". The anthropologist Geertz says that, in trying to understand the native's point of view, the aim is "not to achieve some inner correspondence of spirit with your informants . . . but rather to figure out what the devil they think they are up to" (p. 228).

* * *

"We would rather die than be ethnocentric, but ethnocentrism is precisely the conviction that one would rather die than share certain beliefs."

R. Rorty, 1991

If one assumes, then, that dialogue only takes place between people who recognize "otherness" or difference between them, we should look further to see what is being said about difference. For a number of years the works of Bakhtin and his colleague, Voloshinov, have been studied by scholars from the fields of literary criticism, psychology, philosophy, and communication theory, which has led to the coalescence of a body of theory known as the "dialogical" approach to the understanding of the psychology of human behaviour. Of course, this is a big subject, for which readers should refer to the original writings; however, I want to discuss several of their concepts that I have used to understand organizational behaviour.

De Peuter (1998), writing about Bakhtin's work, says:

I want to suggest that the ideals of autonomy, integration, coherence and authenticity may, like the concept of identity itself, be reconstructed as situated, joint productions defined on the boundary of identity and difference and constituted by the equal forces of synthesis and dispersion, order and disarray. We must fully overcome the Cartesian self/other dichotomy to understand "properties" of selves as liminal, in neither the mind nor the text but *between* interlocutors, real or imagined, and allow for the often silenced centrifugal partners in the dialogue of selfhood. [p. 38]

Sampson (1993) refers to Derrida—"presence is built on absence, identity on difference" (p. 90)—and goes on to say that "Concealed within any positive statement of meaning is an absent, other meaning, suggesting that difference, rather than identity is necessary to our understanding" (p. 89).

Bakhtin argues that communication is in continual tension between contrary forces: the *centripetal forces*, which push towards unity, agreement, and monologue; and *centrifugal forces*, which push towards multiplicity, disagreement, and heteroglossia—or what we might call "multiple voiced-ness". Even a single word embodies this tension. Take, for example, the word "chair"; when this word is uttered, it connects the listener to the concept of "chair" and to some representation of all the chairs he or she has known. The speaker and the listener are in the same communication "ballpark", and this is the centripetal force held within that word.

On the other hand, saying the word "chair" also presents the speaker as a particular, individual person, who is referring to a different set of objects known also as chairs, and this is the centrifugal force. To put it differently, a word connects to a general concept understood by both parties, but it also has a specific meaning offered by the speaker which the listener aims to understand in its particularity. "Each word is a little arena for the clash and criss-crossing of differently oriented social accents" (Voloshinov, 1929, p. 41). "Each word reflects and refracts other words and 'our' words reflect and refract not merely 'our' thoughts, but also the thoughts of those with whom we might be disagreeing" (Shotter & Billig, 1998, p. 16).

I have found that these ideas grab people's imagination powerfully. They speak of the central dilemma of working in organizations, which is that we seek some kind of unity while remaining unique and different from our colleagues. Bakhtin continues beyond this exposition to talk of the necessity of holding onto these contrary forces within ourselves and not retreating into a narrative about ourselves that is built upon unity and understanding—that is, to leave space for disunity, disagreement, and, particularly, lack of understanding of the other. This brings us back to Geertz' memorable phrase: "What the devil to they think they are up to?"

Certainly mystics and philosophers have been saying similar things for eons, and more recently Bateson (1972), a fount of inspiration for systemic thinking, coined the phrase "embrace the contraries", but what Bakhtin particularly contributes to this process is the possibility to see it in action through our use of daily language. He raises our awareness of how words connect to others and how they must also depart from them. He is suggesting that dialogues can be undermined by too much "reflection" of common meanings, and they can also be undermined by too much "refraction" of particular individual meanings.

In a thought-provoking article, Sallyann Roth (1999) addresses this issue by posing the questions: "How can I speak fully when speaking fully may reveal that we simply cannot understand one another?" and "What kinds of actions and contexts encourage me to turn my passion to enquiring about things I do not or cannot understand?" (p. 95). We must be very careful about *too much understanding*.

The organization as a construction

The socially constructed organization is just that: socially constructed. But it is being constructed continuously on a daily, even momentary, basis through individuals interacting with others. The organization never settles into an entity or a thing that can be labelled and described, because it is constantly changing, or reinventing itself, through the interactions going on within it. I have often thought how helpful it would be if agencies placed a sign above their entrance-way which read "under construction".

But the implications of this view challenge much of the current thinking about organizations and should be examined more closely. The traditional view is that there is a *thing* known to us as our agency or organization which we know by observing the patterns of behaviour going on around us. We may then compare our observations with those of others to enrich our pool of experience, and then we create an abstract idea of *"my organization"* in our mind. "This is what Datacom PLC is about", or "This is the kind of organization we are in the mental health team".

But—and this is a very important "but"—the concept of seeing an organization as a social construction *is itself a social construction*. It is dangerous to take a one-sided view of organizations—that is, that they are only social constructions—and lose sight of everything else that an organization "is". An organization is also real people, policies and rules, desks and computers, and budgets that create realities and constraints that become the substance of socially constructed conversations—but the "constructed" world and the "material" world cannot and must not be separated from each other.

So we are in need of some new ideas to help us through this dilemma. I have found some very helpful conceptual tools in the writing of Bruno Latour (1993). He suggests that our experiences reside within three domains. Each domain represents a different aspect of our total experience, and each has its own language and concepts to describe the world around us. I have rephrased his language to explain the domains in the following way: one domain is the domain of the material and scientific, and the language to describe this domain is the language of facts; another is the domain of social construction, whose language is social discourse and rhetoric; and the final domain is that of the political, which uses the language and the operation of power. None of these domains should be explored without reference to the others, but each can be seen as having its own characteristics distinct from the others. What is important to Latour is the way people move amongst these domains and pull discrete elements together.

If we apply these ideas to our current discussion, it becomes easier to place the socially constructed organization in context. It becomes one perspective among a range of perspectives. Latour emphasizes that a fully representative picture of our world must tolerate and move amongst all these domains. What becomes interesting then is not social constructionism exclusively, but the inter-action amongst these domains in our attempts to describe the world. (But that is certainly the subject of another book.)

Organizational culture

Ways of thinking about the organization, whether it be a social construction or a structured entity, are enshrined in the concept of organizational *culture*, which is some composite of the discourses and the activities within an organization which turns it into an abstraction and represents it as a whole. From the social construc-tionist point of view, the great problem with this is that certain experiences are selected over others to become the building blocks of the culture. Someone, or some group, holding some position in the organization is saying: "These are important features of our culture, and they will be enshrined in the discourses that are privi-leged in our organization." When interactional activity becomes abstracted or theorized in this way, we begin to attribute meanings to our interactions on the basis of the way behaviour fits into our preexisting concept of the organizational culture. When this hap-pens, the creative, liberating power of dialogic conversations to create new meanings and, in effect, reinvent the organization is lost.

Bender (1998) puts it thus:

> We are socialised by taking on roles in which our actions are determined to a large degree by the a priori social understand-ing of these roles. In the moment of everyday life, action is mainly repetitive and stable because we have clear ideas of what a situation will entail in the ways we and others are expected to act in it. [p. 186]

This view invariably focuses on the wider role of the organization, the community, or society at large.

I am taking a position that deliberately shifts the emphasis of organizational life away from the static concept of a structured organization and towards a more dynamic concept of evolving discourses that are maintained by dialogic communication, but, in turn, determine which dialogic conversations are possible. I also want to shift emphasis from the organization as a thing that can be named to the organization as an ongoing process created by its members. Culture and discourse influence "from above", but individuals also bring their own particular "identities" to the process of selecting which positions within the available discourses they want to take in order to create dialogue with their colleagues.

Responsibility: who is responsible for a socially constructed organization?

One of the powerful "systemic" tools that a practitioner can bring to her or his work with organizations is the concept of the organization as a whole made up of parts. It leads to the valuable work of clarifying primary tasks and creating mission statements that enable workers to pull in the same direction; I have written about using these concepts elsewhere (Campbell, 1996). However, there is a danger in moving too far down this road. Seeing an organization as a whole made up of parts, as one system, is, after all, a metaphor, albeit a useful one, and one danger of such metaphors is that they can remove the responsibility for individual actions and relocate it in an abstract concept of an *organization* or a *system*. While the social constructionist view is that there is certainly a concept of *the organization* which is created in people's minds through dialogical exchanges, the responsibility for creating this construct must reside with the individuals who are, or are not, in dialogue.

Shotter (1989) has suggested that each of us is responsible for conveying information to others in social contexts, and I have used this idea in my work by discussing with members of an organization their "feedback responsibility" and frequently proposing that each staff member could be appraised for his or her ability to generate dialogic interactions within the agency. My point is that within the constraints of available discourses and the dialogic process, and within the power operations in organizations, individuals must nevertheless take responsibility for their own actions and, thereby, their part in contributing to the social construction of their organization.

Bender (1998), referring to Bakhtin, writes: "We must answer for our own acts by taking into account our unique place in the spatial and temporal moment, our relationships with other people and objects, and the content or product of an act" (p. 190).

* * *

"That which we do not give up easily . . ."

S. Benhabib, 1990

Another interesting perspective on the paradox of being an individual "I" and also a product of social discourse is provided by Benhabib (1990), who suggests that we should think of dialogue as happening between two individuals, "concrete individuals", who, in dialogue, become "concrete others" to each other: "An other who exceeds any conception that can be had of him or her. This is an other with a genuine 'otherness' that calls from us *that which we do not give up easily*: our own self-confident understanding of self, other and world" (p. 119). I find this a very handy concept because it provides a starting point in what can become a "chicken-and-egg" discussion that all too quickly degenerates into a form of relativism: "Everything is true or false because it is relative to everything else."

Placed in the organizational context, many dialogues can be linked together to create a more collaborative, participative perspective on what is going on. In Mary Gergen's terms, this perspective pursues mutual understanding—but not necessarily consensus: "it explores how communication difficulties arise from communication practices that preclude debate and conflict about values, that substitute images and imagery relations for self-presentation and truth claims . . . and that lead to decisions based on arbitrary authority relations" (1999, p. 119).

Before leaving this subject, it is important to relate these ideas to the concept of reflexivity, which has been such an important contribution to the canon of systemic thinking. The concept reminds us to be careful about positioning ourselves either too much "within" or too much "without" the dialogic process. But we should strive to be aware that we are simultaneously autonomous, "concrete individuals" on the one hand, and continually evolving as dialogic partners on the other. The reflexive position helps us

observe ourselves and take responsibility for our part in the process.

Making meaning

I think several ingredients are necessary for these responsible individuals to come together and generate new meanings in dialogue.

1. The first is that each person comes to the dialogue as a *responsible individual*, aware of ideas and actions that he or she wants
to contribute to the construction of new meanings.

2. The second is an *appreciation of difference*: difference amongst
people and points of view must be seen as a resource, not a
threat, which is the wellspring for creating new ideas. Bender
(1998) writes: ". . . dialogue is not only possible but perhaps
enlivened when people *do not* share meaning. What we share is
not as interesting as what we do not share. We cannot learn or
progress from shared meaning; we only learn by encountering
new ideas and acting them out in intersubjective acts" (p. 193).

3. The third is that each person must honour an *obligation to create
meaning* for the other's ideas or actions. The obligation is fuelled
by genuine interest in the other person's ideas. Cecchin (1987)
described a similar process as curiosity, and Bakhtin (1993)
writes about "answerable action" which makes our own behaviour accountable to others for its meaning. Two people will
begin the process if they come together with this obligation to
create some meaning, through dialogue, for the other's actions:
"What the devil do they think they are up to?"

Equity and open dialogue

"We shall call 'true' or 'good' whatever is the outcome of free
discussion—that if we take care of political freedom, truth and
goodness will take care of themselves . . ."

R. Rorty, 1989

Why should someone with power, someone with more to lose than gain, enter into a dialogue that may change their point of view or, more importantly, their position within a social discourse? They shouldn't—and most likely they won't. I do not take the view that genuine dialogue occurs because of good intentions. Rather, in the real world, as I see it, individuals are bound by relationships and discourses that support inequity: rich and poor, men and women, skilled and unskilled. If my aim as a social constructionist consultant or facilitator is to promote genuine dialogue, I must aspire to bring people together in an equitable relationship, to aspire to what Rorty calls the "political freedom" that is the prerequisite for a true dialogue.

This is a tall order for one person, with limited time, in the face of a multifaceted organization; however, as Deetz and White (1999) have said, "voice is not granted by new concepts or elite groups but is demanded by those who have something to say in concrete situations" (p. 119). What I *can* do is create an environment in which all members of the organization can find a "voice" or make demands and then monitor the way the differences, the disagreements, and the conflicts that are bound to arise are managed, or not managed, within the dialogues. Getting dialogue "partners" safely to the discussion is one step; identifying the many ways dialogue can be closed down is another.

Future orientation

Social constructionism, by its very definition, must be oriented towards the future. Essentially, it is a framework that encourages people to be aware that they are continually constructing realities through conversation, and therefore the next thing they say or hear contributes to the process. We are in the process of constructing the future. It is also a hopeful process because it is also saying: "We have it within our power to construct a new reality through conversation."

PART II

A MODEL OF CONSULTATION

CHAPTER TWO

Outline

Although I think that conceptualizing and theorizing are essential for one person to be able to communicate to another, there is a time at which the talking must stop and the ideas must be matched with action. We have now reached the point where we must spell out the ways these ideas are put into practice in organizational work.

My model of consultation to organizations, presented in chapters three, four, and five, is assembled to mirror the stages that the process goes through from start to finish. These six different stages are:

1. getting started;

2. creating a safe environment;

3. creating a focus for work;

4. essential conversations about specific dilemmas;

5. action plans;

6. structures for the future.

Each stage is discussed in detail and is supported by examples (set out in italics) from my recent work. Some exercises are also included, which readers may find will transfer to their own work.

The context for my practice is that I have been ensconced in organizations for many years. A large part of my work is as a course organizer, a trainer, and a therapist in a large postgraduate training centre for the National Health Service in the United Kingdom, which means that I can reflect on all the activities going on around me to validate some of my ideas about how organizations work. I also offer supervision to others about their work. Much of this work is "role consultation" for people who are managing services within larger organizations. My practice takes me into both public- and private-sector institutions, and the differences between these sectors play an important part in my work; however, these have been discussed in detail elsewhere (see Campbell, Coldicott, & Kinsella, 1994) and will not be dealt with here.

I also work directly as a facilitator and consultant for small organizations or work teams. I am often asked to *facilitate* a meeting or "awayday" for an agency. This request is usually made when staff have some aim or purpose for their meeting and they are looking for someone who will "keep them to task", maintain a constructive atmosphere, and see that their goals are reached by the end of the meeting. My work as an organizational *consultant* is different. Here, I am asked to work alongside the organization to solve problems, and to help the staff work more productively (whatever that may mean). This brief is usually more open-ended: the sponsor may have only a vague idea that something is wrong and be even less certain of how to tackle it. In these cases, I tend to have a longer, more collaborative relationship with the organization as a whole.

I am, therefore, drawing here on all my experiences as a long-standing staff member, facilitator, and consultant in order to describe my practice. Part II is intended to be helpful to readers who will be applying these ideas and techniques in any of those three contexts. I have tried to illustrate the general discussion about the application of theory by interspersing some examples of my own experiences. Two longer case studies are presented in Part III.

I do not claim that my work presents the reader with a seamless connection between theory and practice; rather, I would describe my work as *informed by* social constructionist thinking, as well as by systemic thinking. I would also describe it as work that is exploratory but, at the same time, the object of my, and I hope the reader's, scrutiny.

The use of exercises

One of my aims in using a social constructionist approach with organizations is to provide participants with experiences that help them see themselves and the process of constructing the organization differently. This may happen through the work of the consultation itself, but there are occasions when I will ask a staff group to take part in a specifically designed exercise for the purpose of learning about social constructionism by observing their own behaviour during the exercise. The format of exercises must be specific for each group and related to the themes currently being addressed in the consultation. However, I do try to build exercises that contain the following three central aspects of the social construction process:

- Participants present their own ideas (this is ususally done in pairs or in small groups).
- Participants get feedback about their ideas to learn how they are understood or given meaning by others.
- Participants use these new understandings or new meanings to construct, with others, yet further new ideas.

These ideas are similar to models that have been proposed by cognitive theorists (see Willi, Frei, & Limacher, 1993) and dialogue theorists (see Hermans & Kempen, 1993); however, they do not place this process in the organizational context as I am doing in this book.

A few of these exercises are presented in the book in specialist contexts as they are being discussed.

Defining consultation

Much of the work I describe has been done in the context of my role as a consultant, and I think the reader will be better able to relate to my experience if I take the time to discuss what I mean by consultation, particularly the way the traditional models of consultation can be modified or supplanted by the application of social constructionist thinking.

In large and small organizations and in society in general, there are discourses about having outside help. For example, in some cultures organizations see outside help—in the form of management consultants—as indispensable, and a huge budget is set aside each year to pay for these services; however, in many smaller organizations, staff are able to express their concerns more directly and the agency may take a more cautious view of outside intervention. Nevertheless, in my view, employees from all types of agencies are concerned about the prospect of fundamental change in their work roles and responsibilities. In larger organizations, the individual's worry is diffused amongst many employees and a hundred other issues facing the organization, whereas smaller organizations feel the impact of an individual's concern more acutely.

As a member of an organization, one's view of what is going on is limited by the feedback received from the colleagues or clients that are part of one's immediate, proximal network of relationships. The organization as a whole is influenced by feedback from many sources, experienced as coming from many different levels. For example, organizational process is influenced by feedback at the level of individual goals, abilities, or rivalries and by the level of policies, structures, and resources within the organization itself and the higher level of social discourses and government legislation. Feedback comes from many places, but the individual develops a limited and highly selective view of what is "really going on".

A consultant, or any observer of a system, has a different perspective, perhaps a wider view, but certainly a view that will introduce different ideas into the organization, because the consultant is not being organized by the same feedback as are the members of the organization. One consultant may choose to focus on the individual level, another on policies and strategies, but neither can describe "what is really going on"; he or she can only offer a view of a feedback process that employees may be blind to. The consultant offers a different view that can, in the terms I am elaborating here, lead to a new conversation.

It is important to raise these issues, because I find that many organizations look to the consultant to tell them "what is really going on". If a consultant, deliberately or inadvertently, fosters this attitude, the organization may act on the opinion of the consultant but will soon find itself searching for another underlying reality when the organization evolves and throws up another set of problems. In contrast to this is the idea that the organization consists of a series of ongoing conversations about all types of issues at many different levels.

Within the European and American cultures I am most familiar with, there is a recognized distinction between the type of consultation that requires specific information and expertise, and the consultation that evaluates the process of what is going on. Edgar Schein (1969), who coined the term "process consultation", says of the former model:

> There is an assumption that the manager knows what kind of information or what kind of service he is looking for. The success of the consultation then depends on:
>
> a) Whether the manager has correctly diagnosed his needs;
>
> b) Whether he has correctly communicated these needs to the consultant;
>
> c) Whether he has accurately assessed the capability of the consultant to provide the right kind of information or service;
>
> d) Whether he has thought through the consequences of having the consultant gather information and/or the consequences of implementing changes which may be recommended by the consultant. [p. 5]

On the other hand, the process consultant works collaboratively with the manager so that consultant and manager, together, arrive at a diagnosis of the problems and move on to generate a remedy. The expertise of the consultant in the area being explored is less relevant than the skill of involving the client in a collaborative process of diagnosis and remedy. Schein makes the important point that "A consultant could probably not, without exhaustive and time-consuming study, learn enough about the culture of the organization to suggest reliable new courses of action. Therefore he must work *jointly* with members of the organization who *do* know the culture intimately from having lived within it" (p. 8).

While Schein was the first to stimulate a new discourse about consultation, his work was based on communication models and work with sensitivity groups in America in the 1960s. Since then, other models have been introduced, particularly the systemic model of consultation. This uses many of Schein's ideas about collaboration and communication but goes further to look for the interacting patterns that create certain meanings about the organization which prevent it from overcoming obstacles and moving forward. The systemic model has been described elsewhere by myself and various colleagues (Campbell, 1996; Campbell, Draper, & Huffington, 1991; Campbell et al., 1994; Haslebo & Nielsen, 2000). We are now on the verge of new models that will build on social constructionist ideas of language, discourse, dialogue, and power.

CHAPTER THREE

The contract
and the consulting environment

Getting started

"A job well done . . . is a job well started."

Proverb

I have been approached by many people who would like some type of outside help for their organization. The majority of these requests would fit Schein's (1969) model of expert consultation in that they appear to result from a manager and/or staff group deciding what the organization's problems are and what type of person should be invited to help. But I have learned to keep an open mind about these specific requests, for several reasons:

1. I think that it is important for any agency or organization to feel in control of the process of change, and this is particularly so where the process involves bringing in an outside person to kick-start the change process. Certainly, one way to retain control is to present an agenda that is worked out and owned by the staff. Related to this is the issue of whether the consultant is

known and can be trusted to work respectfully with the organization. This is crucial to starting the process and is discussed later.

2. The self-diagnosis is always made within the same frame of thinking that sees dilemmas and problems in the first place. In other words, if the general paradigm within the agency is, for example, that "communication is the key to working well", when the staff feel the agency is not working well they are likely to lay the problem at the door of poor communication. An outsider, on the other hand, might see many fundamental issues at work that are resulting in lack of clear communication.

3. The self-diagnosis is always made within the context of relationships and is therefore a political process. The boss who makes the diagnosis on his or her own will be thinking about his or her relationship to the Board and the managers, or about an abstract notion like a job description. If the staff group together make the diagnosis, the process will be heavily affected by the broader meaning of what is said to whom and by whom. It would be a mistake then to agree to any diagnosis without some exploration and understanding of the underlying relationships being maintained within the process.

Rather than seeing the request for consultation as the result of some diagnostic process, I prefer to see it as the first step, the opening gambit, in a relationship between the organization and me. Most of the requests that have come my way can be categorized in the following way:

1. requests for training;
2. requests for work with relations within a staff group;
3. requests for defining the direction and tasks of the organization;
4. any combination of the above.

Point 4 is not meant to be a joke. If we take seriously the idea that the organization's presentation of itself is merely the first step in making a relationship with the consultant, then as the relationship develops beyond the first step, and as the staff move through a process of change, the needs and requests of an organization may very well shift from one of these categories to another.

I was recently asked to put on a two-day training course for an organization that was a network of consultants who worked with other organizations. I had prepared my lectures, exercises, and handouts for a carefully planned course. However, after lunch on the first day the managing director, who was also the founder of the organization, said, in front of his assembled staff of thirty: "These ideas seem to be very useful, but I think we would all learn more from them if you applied them to us and did a consultation to our organization." Well, I tried to disguise the panic rising through my body and discussed this suggestion with the group, who were in general agreement; so I took a break, put away my comforting handouts, and ventured with them into unknown territory.

In general, however, I find that it is helpful for organizations, as a group, to step back from their daily work, "take stock", and ask the question: "How are we doing?" When they do this, it is inevitable that the need for clear direction and strategy is related to the quality of relationships in the organization. Seeing the organization's presentation through the lens of social constructionism implies that the quality of dialogic communication (or lack of it) affects the way the common vision and strategic plans are generated and sustained.

Negotiating a contract/starting the conversation

The way the organization presents itself is a message to me about two things. The first message is about how they see themselves moving forward. For example, I assume that there have been many voices, some stronger than others, over months or years which have created the constructs of "getting help" or "being clear about where we're going" or "wishing to work better as a team". These "realities" have been socially constructed, and any development within the organization will need to be positioned within the discourse that made these particular constructs possible. I want to get interested in how they came to these conclusions, what the debate was about, who was speaking to whom, and whether there were any alternative views about the way forward that were not accepted. Agencies can come to a clear self-diagnosis because one individual or group has prevailed over another, silencing other voices, in which case help may by needed to bring other voices into the conversation: however, they can also remain uncertain because many voices are supported, in which case help may be called for to discuss the necessity to use power and experience to prioritize agency needs and agree to one direction.

The point is this: unlike a consultant who evaluates the reality of the presenting request, I am trying to place the request in a context of various conversations within the organization which have created these constructs. This is a way of getting inside the process and from there beginning my part in a new conversation that will also become a dialogue that socially constructs some new realities—this time with input from me! I have done this in a number of different ways:

1. In a larger group of twenty or more, it may be possible to meet a "steering group" of three or four people who represent the important groupings in the organization. This gives me the opportunity to hear the different diagnoses and hypotheses about the agency's future. I can also enquire about how the group manages differences and conflict and what they see as obstacles to working together.

2. In a smaller group (say, 5–10 people), it may be possible to meet everyone for a preliminary meeting to discuss consultation. This is a big commitment in time and money for an agency, but it may be the best way to proceed, particularly, I find, when the staff are wary about any decisions being made without their knowledge and prefer to participate in the discussion about consultation.

3. In some organizations, the director or management team, or perhaps a delegated person from within the ranks, will present the agency's thinking about consultation. In this case, the agency has chosen to use the hierarchical structure to link to the outside person, which may fit the culture of the organization.

Any organizational structure places specific constraints on dialogue, and the formal, hierarchical structure often constrains conversations about power, control, and autonomy. Therefore, when the agency is presented in this way, I assume that hierarchy is very important in the context in which the agency operates, and I respect the process for that reason, while also keeping in mind the specific constraints the agency has to manage.

4. "Conversations by proxy" is what I call the process I use when the size of the organization or the distance between us prevents face-to-face conversation. I suggest that the organization should hold certain kinds of internal discussions about the consultation work and then send a summary of the discussion to me. This is a very helpful process in itself, but it particularly gives staff groups the opportunity to discuss outside help in their own way without feeling influenced by the presence of the outside facilitator. In many cases, this is a necessary first step.

I was recently asked to facilitate an awayday with a team distant from my office, that provided a therapy service for the NHS. The group had met together on several occasions to decide that they wanted a consultant, but I needed more information to make some hypotheses. Since I wouldn't be able to meet them before the allocated day, I asked each of them to send me his or her replies to the following three questions:

1. What do you want to get from the awayday?

2. What do you feel are the important issues that need to be addressed in the awayday?

3. What do you think the facilitator may overlook on the day?

Each of the thirteen staff sent their replies to me in separate envelopes. I was aware that I became the "holder of the conversation", but this process and the specific comments the staff sent were invaluable to me in making hypotheses about what conversations we might have on the awayday and, crucially, what "conversations-that-might-not-take-place" I should be carefully listening for.

The second message I listen for from the way the organization presents itself is about how they want to relate to me. What typically happens is that the agency or team decide they want consultation or facilitation from an outsider, and they solicit a few names from amongst themselves. Each name then becomes associated with the staff member who offered it, and the choice of a consultant can become a replaying of agency politics—that is, some staff prefer a facilitator of one persuasion, and other staff a different persuasion.

I am very sympathetic to this process because I have been in the position on several occasions of being in a staff group choosing the "right" facilitator. I have always felt that I wanted an outside person who would clearly hear and respect my point of view and not be swayed and organized by the others. So I imagine that the selection process mirrors the earlier discussion about each person "warranting voice" when they come to a discussion designed to socially construct new ideas for the organization.

To resolve the issue within a group, they may need more information about me and how I might work with the team. I have been asked, for example, to answer some questions over the telephone: "What is my theoretical orientation?", "What other groups have I worked with?", "What if some people do now want to come to the consultation?" and so on. I have been interviewed by directors or managers who present some of their organizational dilemmas to me and then weigh up whether what I say is appropriate and helpful. And I have also been invited to meet a small group from the staff—a vetting committee—to discuss the agency and how a facilitated meeting might be run. The latter has always seemed preferable because I can get some sense of the different points of view represented in the staff group.

The end of the beginning—a contract

Assuming that the opening conversation has led to an agreement between staff and facilitator, it is imperative that the conversation concludes with some mutual understanding about what will be done, and by whom, during the consultation process. From the social constructionist perspective, a consultation or a facilitated meeting will aim to be dialogic such that each party is influenced by the others, but it is a prerequisite that each person enters the dialogue with an opinion, a voice, a profile, so that the others have something to react to. Making a contract is still just a starting point (we might borrow Behabib's phrase and call it a "concrete position"). Although the contract becomes a social construction owned by everyone in the process once the conversation is under way, it is helpful as a place to start from.

Creating a safe environment

Introducing myself

I have found that introductions are very important, because they are the first stage of a dialogue. Everyone in a group has a "voice", and when they—literally—use their voice to introduce themselves, they are—metaphorically—stepping forward to become part of the public domain. Those of us listening to an introduction all belong together as members of the same group, and we are able to claim some ownership of that person who has spoken by the way we listen and give meaning to what he or she says.

I think beforehand and try to introduce myself in a way that sets a tone and defines the context in a particular way. I think about the best way to set an example that will, hopefully, make it possible for this particular group, in their own particular frame of mind, to have safe and fruitful discussions together as a group. For example, in one context it might seem most appropriate to introduce myself in a more personal way, in which case I would introduce myself "warts and all" or talk about my family, or my previous experience as a fighter pilot (just joking!). In another context I might decide that it was more appropriate, depending on my hypothesis or previous thinking about the organization, to introduce myself in terms of people I am most connected to and influenced by in my working life; or I might prefer to present the most challenging dilemma I am currently facing at work. I try to mark the context in a particular way and then ask others to follow suit with similar introductions. Then, while others are introducing themselves, I frequently comment on or ask questions for clarification about certain things that catch my interest, so from the beginning the introductions present opportunities for some dialogue.

An increasingly prominent part of my work with organizations is talking to the participants about how I see organizational life. I discuss, in highly condensed form, some of the ideas about social constructionism which I elaborate in this book. I talk about the value of dialogue and the way language is influenced by social discourse and creates the types of problems that cause so much distress. I discuss our work as an opportunity to have some different experiences together and eventually evaluate whether or how these new experiences can be fitted into the daily life of the organization.

Ground rules for a safe environment

When a local cricket club in England lays out a cricket pitch on the village green, they must decide what rules apply when the ball hits the 300-year-old oak tree or rolls into the duck pond. These become the rules for that particular ground, and all the teams who come to that village abide by them. Similarly, at the beginning of any piece of work I do with an organization, I like to spell out "ground rules" that I hope we will all abide by so that our work together will take place within a safe environment.

The social constructionist perspective has much to offer our understanding of dialogue and the use of language to create new organizational realities, but there seems to be relatively little in the literature about the painstaking efforts required to create a safe environment in the organization before the conversation can start. With regard to creating a safe environment, I find that the systemic concept of *context* is most helpful (see Campbell, 1995).

In organizations we are asked to coordinate our behaviour with other people towards some common goal. These "others" are inevitably different, and this process is stressful and makes employees feel vulnerable. Added to this is the political or power dimension. An organization is an ideal setting for workers to strive for greater influence over others and over the direction in which the organization is moving. We strive to "warrant voice" and have influence, but this is often done at the expense of others' voices and influence. This can all lead to an unsafe environment, and to a dangerous place in which to begin an open dialogue with colleagues.

My priority as a consultant or facilitator is to contribute to the creation of a safe environment in which to begin conversation. To do this I discuss with any group the importance of a safe context and try to spell out what things need to be discussed, as preliminaries, to move towards a safe environment. These stem from my own experiences of what has been helpful to maintain a working context, but they are also adapted to the particularities of the group I am working with. I begin by stating the rules that I use, and the group members usually add some of their own as the discussion develops. The fact that these are discussed, made explicit, and agreed upon gives participants some sense of security as we begin our work together, and I find I spend a considerable amount of time discussing them at the beginning of the work because I can then refer back to agreements we made when for one reason or another the work itself is getting bogged down. The following are the ground rules that I typically introduce in my work.

Talking about safety itself

Simply identifying a safe environment as an important value can be reassuring because I am clarifying my position within a larger discourse about safety for the benefit of all the participants. This also allows others to position themselves and speak about what safety or lack of safety means to them, or how it shows itself, or what specific things they are concerned about.

Making safety a continuous preoccupation

I explain that a safe environment is not something that is just talked about once; each participant must feel that safety is permanently "in place" during our work in order to take the necessary risks of new forms of dialogue. I usually establish as a ground rule the right of anyone to say "I am not feeling safe" at any time during the consultation process; when this happens, I as the facilitator will stop the process to take a step back and look with participants at the wider context of safety. Perhaps new issues of safety have emerged as the work has progressed, but these have not been sufficiently discussed to enable people to feel safe. Time must be set aside to do this.

It may seem to the reader that this is a diversion from the real work of the consultation, but my experience has led me to the conviction that negotiating safety *is* the most important work to be done in the consultation work because it provides the foundation upon which colleagues can begin to take the risk of understanding "other" points of view different from their own.

Shared responsibility

A safe working environment will be socially constructed through the interactions of everyone taking part in the consultation. As far as I am concerned, both facilitator and participants are responsible for creating a safe environment and for making the work successful. If at the end of the work—whether it be one day or one year—people are not satisfied, they must carry some responsibility for the dialogues that they did, or did not, take part in. I try to delineate the different responsibilities between participants and myself. While I am responsible for maintaining the safe environment, for drawing out key issues that require discussion, and for ensuring that we reach some closure at the end, they are responsible for participating in the dialogic conversations necessary to construct new images of their relationship and of the organization as a whole.

I have borrowed from Shotter a concept that I call "feedback responsibility"—that is, each participant is responsible for deciding what feedback he or she wants to give others in order to stimulate a dialogic conversation with the potential of influencing others' ideas and, in turn, changing his or her own ideas. If every member of the organization is willing to take this responsibility, new ideas will emerge; if they are not willing or able to "sign on" to this responsibility, I would, as I have said, assume that the environment is not safe enough and take a step back to consider with them "what needs to be discussed first to make the environment safer for people to be able to work together."

In this situation, I have found two ideas extremely helpful. The first is to make the distinction between the *work that the organization will do with me* and *creating the right environment before the work can be done*. While I certainly see these activities as part of the same process (i.e. we are certainly working to create a new organization while we are building a safe environment), making a distinction that enables people to see a progression from one stage to the next also helps all of us to feel that we can have some control over the process and move it forward or backward in time as we desire.

The second idea, which I have adapted from the behaviourists and solution-focused therapists, is to think with participants in terms of "making one small change" in order to kick-start a change process rather than thinking that one has to change an entire organization. In fact, I see my role as a facilitator as someone who helps get the process of change started through different types of conversations, and then helps set up the apparatus that enables the organization to observe and adjust the changes as they take place—that is, to create an "organizational awareness".

Taking risks

So far there has been a lot of thought and discussion about the safe environment, but within that context people must also be able to face up to others to give them feedback or, alternatively, listen openly to others' feedback about themselves. In other words, they must be prepared to do things that they have not done before: they must take risks. I make the point during this discussion that, as a facilitator, I too will be taking risks, by trying something new, departing from the agenda to follow my own instincts. Having made this point, I can then comment on the occasions when, during the work, I think I am taking a risk and why. Participants love getting involved with these comments.

Once again, by having this discussion as one of the ground rules I try to make risk-taking both acceptable and "safe enough".

A colleague, Barry Mason, has used the concept of helping clients to work in a context of "safe uncertainty" (1993). I make a different emphasis by suggesting that the work will move forward more quickly if and when people feel able to take risks in their conversations with others. Once this is placed squarely on the agenda for our work, I can refer back to it from time to time by, for example, asking people whether they have just taken a risk by saying what they just said.

Allowing oneself to be influenced

Although listening to others seems the simplest part of having a dialogic conversation, I think it is the hardest. For this reason, I set aside time to highlight, perhaps warn, perhaps encourage, the importance of the listening process. I emphasize the ability to listen in such a way that one's own beliefs, assumptions, impressions, whatever, are laid open to being changed through the process of understanding where someone else is coming from. This is a form of suspended belief, but at the root must lie a trust that something better emerges from shifting one's point of view towards understanding the other's. This is a very tall order. I do not expect everyone to move in this direction, but I do find that discussing these possibilities and allowing for these possibilities goes a long way towards building the most conducive environment.

My own thinking about listening has been influenced by the creative and courageous work done by the Public Conversation Project in Massachusetts (Becker et al., 1995).

A space to think and a space to act

Work with an organization must tread a fine line between stepping back and thinking and theorizing on the one hand, and getting involved with others to create new conversations about real issues on the other. One typical format for organizational work is the "awayday", in which an entire agency goes away, preferably to a tranquil setting in the countryside, leaving the pressures of the office behind. As a facilitator I have found that this tension between thinking and generating new conversations can be very creative, so I discuss with the group the value in doing both the thinking and acting while we are together. For an away-day, for instance, I frequently divide the time between a reflective phase in which participants are invited to share what they are experiencing in the organization, or unresolved issues from the past, and an active phase in which the participants are asked to have certain conversations and to commit themselves to specific structures and strategies that will carry them into the future.

Once again, this topic of discussion, like the others, helps participants learn more about me and my values, helps us all get "on the same wavelength" in terms of the process of the work together, and sets a framework around the work which helps us all to feel more secure and able to depart from our established views and perhaps to take risks, knowing that there are rules or values or structures underpinning the work as a whole.

I also invite the participants to comment on the process of the consultation itself. There will be times during the work when I will stop and say: "Let's step back and look at the process: how are we doing?" The consultation or facilitation is a learning opportunity for everyone—a time and space to reflect. I use the metaphor of thinking on two levels at the same time—the level of the *content* of what we are discussing, and the level of *process* of how we are going about it—and I invite everyone to employ this dual-level thinking and comment on it, as they please, throughout the work. To acknowledge the thinking that is done, I tell the group that I will leave time at the end for them (and me) to share thoughts with the group.

Confidentiality

In order to support the distinction between the real world in which staff members have to work with each other on a daily basis and the reflective world of the original work, it may be helpful to include among the ground rules an agreement about confidentiality. Participants will feel safer if it is agreed that the things said during the consultation work should not provoke any actions to be taken outside the consultation work itself. Instead, I find it helpful to designate time during the work to consider specifically which actions will be put into effect and by whom on the basis of the discussions that have taken place in the consultation work.

Respectful behaviour

In some agencies struggling with high levels of mistrust and tension, there is frequently a fear that the consultation process will blow the lid off the smouldering feelings and make things worse. This can be tricky. One potential pitfall is that the facilitator may back away from the conflict and facilitate work that is avoidant and superficial. On the other hand, I have learnt over the years that techniques based on "letting all your feelings out" can be very counterproductive, and I usually discuss this dilemma with the group in terms of my previous experiences and expectations. I have learnt that the conflicts have to be discussed, but that this should be done using respectful language that supports professional behaviour towards one's colleagues. I have also learnt that balancing the discussion between what has happened in the past and how people want to do things differently in the future has proven to be an effective way to resolve conflicts in organization.

Introducing the consultant's opinions

For years I have used a model of systemic thinking that emphasizes the need for a therapist or consultant to articulate her or his own thoughts about the group that she or he is working with. Known as hypothesizing, this technique involved using the consultant' own thinking as a means, not for testing the truth of one's observations, but as a way for the consultant to remain fully engaged, listening carefully, and curious to learn more about the clients (see Cecchin, 1987). But now, in the framework of a social constructionist approach, it is time to re-visit the vexed question of the status of the consultant's own ideas. Are they true? Are they helpful? When, if at all, should they be shared? Do they simply consolidate the power relationship between consultant and client?

I am placing this discussion at the beginning of the consulting process because anyone working with an organization will form his or her own thoughts from the moment of the first contact—whether a letter, a telephone call, or a meeting—and the question is, what to do with these thoughts? I now have years of experience and I am asked by agencies to offer my observations and opinions, yet the things I say should be seen as only one-half of a dialogic process between consultant or facilitator and client. This is a skewed relationship in that most participants would agree that there is more consultative experience or more ability to take an overview residing in one side of the dialogue than in the other. This skewed relationship will constrain participants and lead the dialogue in a particular direction; however, once the dialogue is begun with the first comments, it will take on an unpredictable direction of its own. And it is as this is happening that a consultant must *loosen the grip of his or her own opinions* and become curious about why the dialogue proceeds as it does—from "What the devil do they think *they* are up to?" towards "What the devil do *we* think *we* are up to?"

I have certainly made mistakes at both poles of this process. I was working with a larger (50 employees) organization in a country abroad and struggling to get a grasp of how the management really worked, yet I felt pressure to make some illuminating comments about what was "really going on". The more I felt this pressure, the more I retreated into a safer, observing, "let's wait and see" position. When I finally felt that I had painted myself into a corner, I was able to step back and formulate some ideas based on the process of what had been happening to me throughout the day. This led me to speculate with the group about the feeling of pressure that they might experience and the competitive, rivalrous feelings amongst staff. Many of them liked these ideas, and we went on to explore how the organization "managed for high standards" without creating unhelpful pressure and competitiveness.

On the other hand, I was asked to facilitate an awayday with a smaller agency for which I had been offering consultation to the director on his own for several months. I felt more confident that my ideas about the organization and how it should use the awayday were "right", and I moved too quickly to steer things down my own path. I felt that my ideas were not readily accepted but were met with counter-proposals, to which I had to adjust. The experience left me feeling that I should have spent more time negotiating with the whole group (8 people) instead of "falling in love with my own ideas".

So, my point is that although the consultant's opinions are crucial to setting a dialogue on its course, we must then allow the dialogue to move in its own direction and we must learn from observing this process. One of the social constructionist writers has said that a truth is merely a pause in an ongoing conversation. I find this idea very helpful. Our opinions are like road signs at a fork in the road: we offer them to the travellers and then follow them down the path they choose to travel though their dialogue.

CHAPTER FOUR

Focus and action

Creating a focus for work

When given the opportunity to change things within their own organization, most people will have an idea of what it is like for them in the present (point A) and what they want things to be like in the future (point B). So, in its simplest terms, I begin by assessing with the group what point A looks and feels like and what point B looks like and how they will know when they have arrived. This can be done in a number of ways, from individual interviews, to postal questionnaires, to small or large group discussions, depending on the constraints and culture of the organization.

> Several years ago, I was invited to offer consultation to the management team of a housing agency that consisted of different departments representing different aspects of the agency's work: finance, personnel, vetting applicants, housing stock, and so on. There were big differences in each manager's perception of the agency, and there was also some bad feeling about the way the

agency was managed. In discussion with the director, we de-cided that I would interview each of the seven managers, at hourly intervals, during one day. I would then pool the informa-tion and draw my own conclusions about what was going on, and this would form the basis of a one-day seminar with the management team. This was a fascinating exercise because as I saw the agency through each person's eyes—fully convinced that each manager was "right", or at least justified in their views—I slowly acquired an overall picture that gave some meaning to their difficulties.

However, I wasn't completely satisfied with the subsequent one-day seminar, for two reasons. First, I think I moved too quickly into discussing the "big picture" of their agency and.neglected to give them sufficient opportunity to talk amongst themselves—or, in the jargon of this book, to have a dialogue—about the differ-ences I had encountered in the individual interviews. It was as though I moved too quickly to an overarching connecting theme without taking everyone through the process of discussing differ-ence and potential conflict.

The second reason was that there was pressure on me during the day, as there frequently is, to design structures and procedures to make the agency function more effectively. I made the mistake of not pausing in the second half of the day to review the expecta-tions, and I feel that there was some frustration amongst the staff when we finished. As I look back on this work, I realize the necessity of negotiating both the ends and the means of a semi-nar with the group before proceeding—a very valuable lesson.

I have learnt from my own experiences that there is often a culture conflict between a consultant who is an outsider assuming the privileged position of standing back and commenting on the process, versus the staff members immersed in the organization and obliged to get their work done to a standard and perhaps even a deadline. It is often helpful to discuss the culture clash and some of the latent feelings about consultants (often a mixture of trepida-tion and disdain). I find it helpful to discuss the previous experi-ences they have had with consultants, and the experiences that the group had in coming to the decision to invite a consultant, or me personally, into their organization. I know, on occasions, that I have made the mistake of overlooking this conflict in my eagerness to engage the staff and get started on the "real work", but when it is not discussed it has a tendency to surface at a later stage of the work.

Through the appropriate discussion between the consultant and the staff, the participants can create some understanding of what can and cannot be achieved in their work together. The approach and techniques of the consultant need to be matched with the aims and the expectations of the organization. And this all has to be placed in the context of time, money, and resources.

I was recently approached by a multidisciplinary mental health team who had set aside a fixed amount of money to pay for a facilitator for a staff awayday. (Generally, I am careful about offering awaydays to organizations unless I feel the organization has built the infrastructure, such as meetings, to consolidate the changes initiated during the awayday.) I felt that there was a risk that the awayday would become an isolated event, productive, perhaps, in terms of providing new understandings but unconnected to ongoing organizational development, so I discussed with the manager the possibility of spreading the work across four meetings at monthly intervals. It gave all of us the chance to think about the agency over time in more depth, and to monitor at each meeting what was happening to the process of change. At the end of each session, tasks were set to be reviewed at the next meeting. When the work was completed, the follow-up forms from the staff supported the popularity of this format.

The problem-determined system

Social constructionism has been influenced by the concept of the problem-determined system, articulated by Anderson et al. (1986). They proposed that through a series of relationships and conversations within a multidisciplinary team of professionals working together on a difficult mental-health case, a system evolves around the shared idea of a problem. Without "the problem" they would not exist as an interacting system, but this fact can also make it difficult for the group to see anything but problems when they observe the case. The strength of the ongoing process of social construction within this system can make it difficult to see the case differently—that is, to see solutions in the place of problems.

Agencies and organizations seeking help share much in common with these "problem-determined systems". Their ongoing conversations about their work take place within problem-saturated discourses. Problems become like spectacles that colour the way the agency and other people are seen, and the broader picture of the agency's values and activities can become lost.

> In preparation for a recent awayday with a small agency experiencing problems in staff relations, I asked the group to send me written comments about what they thought should be attended to on the awayday. These are some of their comments:
>
> - "A sense of balance between the levels of satisfaction and dissatisfaction within this department."
>
> - "How much ability, goodwill, creativity we can and do generate between us sometimes."
>
> - "The possibility that you, as a facilitator, might overlook the good points about the department."
>
> - "The tendency amongst us to feel unappreciated and underrewarded."

I was struck by the staff's own wish to be appreciated for what they are trying to do.

I have found on many occasions that it is difficult for a staff group to tackle some of their organizational dilemmas if they are feeling demoralized. Talking about the demoralization can be helpful, but it may not lift them to a state of mind in which they can take the risk of having different conversations with each other and challenging their beliefs. This resonates with the work of Cooperrider and Srivastra (1987), who have built organizational work around their concept of *appreciative enquiry*. This approach, which is growing in popularity, emphasizes the things an organization does well, and the things that employees feel good about, and builds on these *strengths* rather than focusing on *problems*. I have found that this approach is very effective for engaging with a new group and getting the consultation work started. I think that it is easy for an outsider to underestimate how demoralized many groups feel when they are in the grip of ongoing stress at work and they have tried and failed many times to "pull themselves up by their own bootstraps".

When the environment feels "safe enough" for all of us, I move the group to the next stage of the process. This stage fundamentally poses the question: "Now that we are ready for work, what do you want to be different in your organization?" We then have conversations to find out where to begin focusing our attention.

I find that the most valid answer to the question—that is, the answer that most often leads towards significant change for the organization—does not arise immediately. Rather, it needs to be teased out by encouraging individuals to reflect on their own personal experiences. If these are not reflected in the final focus, the changes will not stick (see Campbell, 1996). As individuals begin to speak, I listen carefully for the interconnecting themes or patterns.

Here it is helpful to remember that problems are socially constructed through conversations based on the discourses available to the organization. It is these discourses and these conversations that determine what is a problem. "Discourse" is not a friendly word, and I see eyes glazing over whenever I use it, so when I am talking to a staff group I often prefer to use the word "values". I am referring to a similar part of the social constructionist process—that is, what the basic beliefs are within the organization that give meaning to the way experiences are interpreted. It is these values that are the bedrock of the social constructionist process, and I frequently make space and time to discuss the underlying values that people have about their work: What is the purpose of their work? What do they think makes a good "job of work'"? What do they think a worker "should" feel about his or her work? If one can explore these values or discourses, the participants become connected to fundamental beliefs that govern attitudes, but also the consultant gets an idea of where differences may lead to painful misunderstandings and, most crucially, make it impossible to socially construct new meanings.

Socially constructing problem patterns

I also have an obligation to represent my opinions within this conversation. No consultant—or therapist, for that matter—can be neutral. We can merely try to be aware of our particular biases and take responsibility for the way we construct the world around us. Our own experiences can be used to present ourselves as real, "concrete individuals" bringing difference and diversity into a dialogue, as long as we do not hold too tightly to our opinions, turning them into "truths". As the Milan team of family therapists used to say: "We must not fall in love with our own hypotheses."

So, perhaps we can have a brief "flirtation" with our hypotheses. For example, there are a number of patterns I have observed over many years of working with organizations which, "in my opinion", lead to difficulties that organizations define as problems and are frequently unable to de-construct. I am not referring to personal qualities, which also play a big part in the construction of organizational problems; rather, I am referring here to the interactional patterns that are constructed through the social process in the organization and then get labelled as "patterns" or "problems" (as I am doing right now) that are experienced as painful and often seen as insoluble. I put forward these ideas not as causes of organizational dysfunction, but as patterns of behaviour, or attitudes of mind, or values, or discourses that are difficult to let go of and therefore make it difficult for individuals to construct new ways of seeing their relationships and the organization as a whole. The following are such examples:

1. *Criticism and blame.* This is a crippling process in organizations, where so much of ourselves is on constant display and we are being judged against organizational standards for doing things well. People trapped in these feelings are compelled to try to "win" or "do better" and have little left over to build new relationships.

2. *Rivalry.* When people see the organization as the forum for getting ahead at others' expense, they may get locked into a rivalry that consigns the organization to second place.

3. *Lack of support.* Many workers back away from difficult challenges because the organization has not found the means to

support them in managing the resulting stress. Backing away leads to demoralization and also slows down the progress of the organization.

Menzies Lyth (1988) was a pioneer in identifying the effects of personal anxieties in the workplace. She observed that nurses on a hospital ward had strong feelings about the death of their patients, but, because this was not discussed on the wards, the nurses kept their feelings to themselves and were unable to work well as a team.

This observation has been borne out in much of my work with agencies that draw on the emotional resources of their staff to carry out their tasks. Such agencies do need to provide the means for staff to talk together about the emotional impact of their work and what the expression of feelings may mean to the organization.

4. *Unable to see the influence of one's labour.* Being able to see the effect of one's work, and believing that it makes a contribution, however small, to the life of the organization is the glue that holds the individual to the organization.

5. *Unclear about how to work.* Simple as this may sound, many employees suffer from not knowing precisely what the organization wants from them and whether their work is at one with the vision of and direction in which the organization is moving.

6 . *Ambivalent feelings about leadership.* Many people in positions of leadership are unclear or ambivalent about using authority in the workplace; from the other side, employees may be uncomfortable surrendering part of their own authority to support that of someone in a higher position. Authority and leadership can be undermined in myriad ways, and it is wise always to explore this issue in consultation work.

But the status of these opinions within a social constructionist framework is that they are hypotheses that will guide my listening and observing into certain areas and not others. Since I cannot hear everything said to me, and since I am biased in particular ways, I will be listening and looking for evidence that these themes might usefully be de-constructed and re-constructed through the process of dialogue and conversation. These hypotheses may lead to what I call "essential conversations".

Social constructionists frequently have to answer the charge that they are guilty of rampant relativism (and so they should!), whereby nothing is true and the consultant never has to take a stand for or against one particular reality. But in my view this is a misreading of the position I am trying to clarify in this book. I certainly use the idea that certain patterns of behaviour are going on that cause "real" problems for an organization and that these patterns may be the result of assumptions that people are both aware and unaware of. These are realities that I believe should be explored for the benefit of the agency. But when I say this, I try to acknowledge to myself (which is not always easy to do in the heat of the moment) that I am simply taking one position, or following one hypothesis, that has been socially constructed by me, my background, experience, and so on. The interesting thing about pursuing these patterns in organizational work is to discover what exchanges or conversations have happened that led people to those assumptions. For example: "That's an interesting idea—what, or who, has influenced you to think that way?"

Sharing values

I agree with those writers who claim that our sense of who we are, and how we see our organization, is *preceded* by meanings created by cultural traditions and values (see Hermans & Kempen, 1993). In my experience, a consultation may founder because decisions have been made without exploring the values that support people's views of the organization, and when the decisions have to be re-visited in a new context, the staff are in disarray because their differing values lead them to different interpretations of the situation they all find themselves in.

> *I facilitate fortnightly meetings with a group of six GPs who run their own practice as a partnership. They are continually having to respond to government directives about new directions in health care, but they are also having to decide the best ways to organize their practice to pay their salaries. Our meetings often*

focus on how to prioritize the various options for spending their time: should they supervise trainee doctors? establish more screening clinics? give time to research projects? As a result of this focus, they produced a list of core values (such as high quality of care, fair and equitable practice, GP training and teaching, strong communicating links), all of which are now fixed to the noticeboard. They are now able to say more clearly: "If we are committed to providing a comprehensive community service, we should say 'No' to this request to do research."

I particularly want to stress the "sharing" aspect of this first stage of work, as this is an important prerequisite for the conversations that lead to the social construction of new ideas about the organization. When members of an organization hear the values that their colleagues think underpin their work, they can begin to have a dialogue from two positions.

Changing values

Some agencies do not articulate problems as such, but, rather, seek help to face a changing future. This is a common phenomenon in large public-sector institutions such as the NHS, social services, or local education departments, which are frequently reorganized, ostensibly to save money and improve services. This means that any team or smaller service within a department may suddenly be told "from above" that certain changes are imminent. If the agency is small, there is more likelihood that they will not have participated in the decision-making process, which would be carried out by larger groups (or "cost centres") wielding bigger budgets. This makes staff feel insecure, unsupported, and angry.

In this context, a consultation is an opportunity for the agency to gather together and speculate about what is happening around them and whether the value base that the agency has established in the past will equip them for the future.

For example, one such agency, which was established upon values of high-quality psychotherapy services is facing budget limitations as it tries to expand its service to meet the changing demands for services and the changing sources of funding. As a result, budgets have been allocated within the agency to smaller service groups who have no previous experience managing a budget. This leads to a fundamental clash of values between "Doing the professional work one was trained for to a high standard" and "Learning to manage a budget to do the professional work within financial limits". The agency is slowly embarking on a series of interdisciplinary meetings to discuss the changing values around them and the way they want to redefine their own values to adapt best to the changing environment.

EXERCISE 1: DISCUSSION OF VALUES

Every organization is socially constructed through action, the performative function of language. Therefore, it is essential that values are discussed as the bases for action.

I ask people to discuss the values that they believe are guiding them to do what they do or say what they say in the workplace. Since a value is a metaphorical concept and can remain in a person's head, I want to tease it out to learn how values are demonstrated in each person's behaviour.

In such an exercise, it is crucial that each person has a voice to speak and others are able to listen and be influenced. Therefore, the size and safety of the group must be considered. I find that people feel some inhibition about speaking in groups larger than five or six, so I prefer to do this exercise in groups of three or four (and sometimes, in small meetings, in pairs).

1. In groups of three, each person is asked to take it in turn to speak to the other two, who are asked to listen until their turn comes: "Think of the most important things you do in your work in this agency and share with the others what values underpin your work" or "what are the fundamental values that underlie the way you do your work in this agency?"

2. When each person has had a chance to speak, they are asked to comment on what they have heard from the other two. A good question to stimulate this feedback is: "What other ideas do you have about how you understand the values un-

derpinning X's behaviour?" It is important at this stage not to blunt the differences that may emerge. These differences are the touchstone that will, eventually, produce a socially constructed idea of values, but if one moves too quickly towards synthesis, the creative tension provided by difference will be lost.

3. The final phase of this exercise is the opportunity to synthesize the different ideas about values from the individual groups into one picture that the group as a whole can identify as values of their organization.

I frequently find that individuals within a team articulate different values for similar work. For example, an organization consisting of a network of consultants revealed a gendered difference in the values underpinning their client relationships. One group claimed that they were "problem-solvers" above all else, while another group aimed to model fair and open relationships amongst all staff in their own consultation work. When this happens, it can lead to a very productive discussion about how the organization wants to manage this difference in the future so that both groups feel that their values are incorporated in the work of the agency.

Connecting to the outside world

Having shared the values in the organization, I also find it helpful to create a systemic picture of what conversations the organization is engaged in that feed the discourse they have about themselves. That is, I would ask myself: "What other parts of the system or wider network are giving the feedback about how they should 'be' as an organization? Who tells them they are doing things well or not so well? How do they learn these things?" This means that I need to place the organization in its wider context: the outside world.

A consultation such as an agency awayday is an opportunity for the agency as a whole to hear a shared, and hopefully coherent, version of what is happening in the outside world and to spend time together redefining their value base. One effective way of doing this is to ask a leader or management team to begin the day with a presentation, which then leads to further discussion.

I facilitated an awayday with a psychology service attached to a large hospital trust that was soon to be taken over by another trust and had been asked to merge its services with the neighbouring psychology service. The head of the service had been involved in meetings to discuss the merger but had not had time to bring her 20-strong staff group into the picture or to plan together for the future. The latter was the purpose of the awayday. I asked her to make a brief presentation of what she had been discussing in her meetings and the dilemmas that she felt were facing the service about its future. I hoped that these dilemmas would challenge the current value base and prompt the group to create new values through dialogue and discussion.

She ended her five-minute talk by posing three questions:

1. *"Although we are the smaller service, how can we influence the shape of the new service?"*

2. *"What values and practices do we want to hold on to as we merge?"*

3. *"What can we gain from the new department to help us do our own work better?"*

Another approach to positioning an organization in the outside world is to see it as part of a network that includes other agencies who are in some way connected. I have found Guba and Lincoln's (1989) discussion of "stakeholder" groups very helpful in developing my own approach. I try to identify which other groups are interested in the future of the organization (say, "Agency X") I am consulting to. Groups such as referrers, paymasters, client groups, professional bodies, the government, and the staff group itself, for instance, are all interested, in their own way, in the future of Agency X. The discussion then leads on to defining how the work of Agency X connects to the interests and preoccupations of the other groups. This is a helpful process not only for positioning Agency X, but also for doing strategic planning for the future.

Exercise 2: Connecting to the outside world

Within the framework of social constructionism, the intention of this exercise is to facilitate conversations (either real or imaginary) with other groups that have an interest in the workings of Agency X. This helps the staff of Agency X to see themselves as part of a much larger system, and it opens the way for a dialogue with these other groups about the best way for these agencies to work together for the good of all concerned.

1. I begin by asking Agency X to identify the groups that are connected with the agency. I use the term "stakeholder" for any group that has a "stake" in the agency's work or its future. This should be limited to a small number of the most relevant groups, say 7 or 8, so that the exercise does not become too complicated. These groups are written up on a flipchart for all to see.

2. Each group is discussed in turn in response to the questions:

   • "How does this group connect to the work of Agency X?"

   • "How could you develop your relationship with each group to enable you to do the work of Agency X better?"

   • "How could the other groups support your relationship with the one group we are focusing on?"

   This discussion can be done hypothetically, but it can also be done through a role-play where members of Agency X take the part of, and speak for, these other "stakeholder" groups; on occasion, I have also invited representatives from the stakeholder groups to take part in such an exercise. This can have a powerful, galvanizing effect on Agency X.

3. If the aim of the consultation is to do strategic planning for the future, then plans should be made on the basis of these conversations and tested out by soliciting a response to the plans from the stakeholder groups, either through the hypothetical discussion or by talking to the stakeholders directly. This pattern can be repeated as often as needed because each strategic plan needs to be tested against the reaction of other groups and then revised and tested again.

Essential conversations about specific dilemmas

Whereas "creating a focus" is a broader, more exploratory phase of the consultation, the next stage identifies specific issues that can be discussed in the form of structured conversations. At this stage, social constructionism is put into action. Rather than calling this process the "socially constructed conversation", which is a cumbersome piece of jargon, I prefer to refer to these as "essential conversations" to highlight their specificity and importance in the process of change. They are conversations with a purpose, which is to enable people to open up conversation, explore alternative views, and gradually move towards a new construction of the issue at the heart of the conversation.

I use the systemic concept of the whole consisting of many interacting parts as the basis for creating conversations within the organization. I tend to see individuals as parts who interact to create teams or services or departments; the teams or services that interact to create the organization; and the organization that interacts with its wider environment to remain a viable, recognized system. Systems theory proposes that each part has some boundary around it that distinguishes it from other parts, and these systems are held together by the maintenance of these boundaries. (Systems theory has moved from its origins in the 1950s and 1960s and now formulates that these boundaries themselves are relative to the observer, who cannot stand apart from the system that he or she is observing.)

I link systems theory with the theory of social constructionism by proposing that it is conversation across the myriad boundaries that maintains organizations as viable, generative systems. But what do I mean by boundary? This itself is a construct created by someone who observes difference and who needs, or wants, to acknowledge the difference—someone who wants to be able to say, "This is me, that's the other" or "This is good, that is bad" or "This is an administrative task, that is a professional task". I take a functional rather than structural view of boundaries (although these are often overlapping)—that is, an observer in an organization will see certain differences and define them with the concept of boundary because doing so helps this person function in some particular context. For example, it will be seen in many teams that one can get tasks done more efficiently if they are delegated to different people, each with a boundary around his or her job description.

The essential boundary that allows the consultant or facilitator to work with an organization is the very difference between consultant and organization, and this is the place to start. To reiterate what was said in the previous section, negotiating the contract to do work can be conceptualized as conversation, the aim or function of which is to socially construct the concept "consultation" so that both sides are happy and the work can progress on the basis of common premises.

The aim or function of the conversation I must have with the organization is to continuously construct together through dialogue some shared notion of a consultation process. I will contribute to my side of the dialogue by the way I behave, the ideas I present, and the people I speak to. I will be socially constructing "facilitation" by the themes I respond to and the balance I strike between supporting and challenging staff. For example, I have struggled with some groups because they were expecting a style from me that was supportive and positive whereas I exposed too many underlying tensions amongst staff; I have also made mistakes in the other direction, with a group expecting hidden motives to be revealed whereas I was moving them towards building new relationships for working together in the future.

Irrespective of how I have been asked to work with an organization, because I am an outsider I will have some capacity to take an overall view. Coupled with this, I have some years of experience with other organizations that I can draw on to place the current organization in context. And I have an obligation, as a consultant, to maintain this ongoing conversation through sharing ideas and actions, as well as through my speaking and silence, so that the "consultation relationship" is continually being constructed, or perhaps de-constructed and re-constructed. This is the basis of the social constructionist model of organizational consultation.

Entering the dialogue

The dialogue between me and the organization is a delicate balancing act. Many organizations are not used to a social constructionist model: they expect to be told what is going on and then to make the necessary adjustments. I want to respect this tradition but at the same time to introduce new ways of thinking. I am trying to convey a way of having conversation in which creating dialogue and mutual influence is more important than winning people over to your point of view. I encourage people to think about how to have a conversation rather than sharpening and refining their own thinking, for, when it works, the dialogic process itself can refine thoughts and supply the intellectual rigour that the organization will need to make good decisions. As I see it, this approach is not about agreement, compromise, and fuzzy thinking: it is about listening carefully for difference, allowing oneself to be influenced by dialogue, and observing the process.

I put my own opinions into the process in several ways:

1. I try to explain where my opinion has come from. For example, did I have a conversation with the director, or overhear a comment during a coffee break, which clarified my own thoughts? This demystifies my opinions, places them in a context, and makes them more sensible and understandable.

2. I try to comment on the status of my opinion. Is it something that just occurred to me and can be taken lightly, or is it something based on hours of thinking about the organization? If the latter, I hope it will be given careful consideration. Related to this is what the opinion means to me. Is it something I feel passionately about? Is it something I hope they will take away from the work we are doing? But such strong statements should also then be qualified so that they do not assume an importance above and beyond the ongoing dialogue.

3. I try to make the point that although opinions are extremely important for generating dialogue, they are not *necessarily* important in themselves. So I might say: "I have this particular idea, but I'm really interested to know what you think about it." I like to think of opinions as interventions to kick-start a process, rather than as ends in themselves.

The reason I have gone on at such length about the subject of my opinions is that the things I say and do represent the beginning of a dialogic process. I want to become as aware of this process as possible, and I want to model the process for the organization as a whole.

Essential conversations

Returning now to the organization as a nesting of Russian dolls, each a part to the larger whole, I begin this phase of the consultation process by asking myself and all the participants one key question:

> "At this stage in the consultation, what conversations need to take place, across which boundaries, with whom, and about what?"

We discuss this together as a means of addressing any problem or area that needs development. I expect the participants to discuss and decide together where they think the priorities lie for their organization. They may focus on boundaries between the organization and the outside world, looking at ways of improving interactions with other agencies.

For example, I worked with a mental health team who felt very much a "Cinderella" service within their community, losing out in recognition and resources. For them it became clear that the essential conversations, at this early stage, were on the boundaries between (a) the management of their service and (b) their service and similar services in the community. We developed some ideas about how the work of this team could collaborate and enhance the work of other teams, using the stakeholder exercises discussed above; we drew up a list of what was required of management to develop the service in this way; and, finally, we devised strategies for deciding which meetings should be attended by whom in the team to put these ideas forward and begin some type of dialogue.

Alternatively, the participants may decide that the boundaries within the organization itself are a greater priority. This is the case when people feel unhappy about relationships in the staff group. Once again, I would apply the same question: "What conversations need to take place across which boundaries, with whom, and about what . . . at this stage in the consultation?" but in this case the answer is different, it is something like: "The staff group need to have conversations with each other about the differences and lack of respect that have grown amongst them."

An example of a conversation at this level is that of a psychology service that offers individual counselling and psychotherapy to various clients in the NHS. As they talked together (a group of 10) about respect, it became clear that they did respect each other's skills but did not have the time or opportunity to work together in groups in order to develop closer collaborative relationships. This had not been possible because the culture dictated that individual therapy should be a priority. The tension in the group seemed to be related to their construct of "team", which was that the whole service should see itself as a team; however, this was impossible, because some workers were part-time and had no time to spare for team projects, whereas others did not have an interest in such projects. These thoughts prompted me to lead the group into focused, "essential conversations" that I hoped would help them re-construct their idea of being a team. I asked them to discuss in pairs, "How they could see themselves as a team which allowed for greater opportunities for people to work together". From these conversations, the group established that some people would work together on collaborative projects whereas others would not join these projects.

As I discussed in chapter one, equity is a key issue affecting how well small teams function. My own experience is that organizational life stirs so many feelings about competition and rivalry and fairness that things must be seen to be fair for people to trust each other and work well together. I have asked many teams to have conversations about examples of inequity in the workplace and what the organization could do to reduce them. One specific area in which the question of equity is frequently raised is the different tasks and salary levels between professional and administrative staff.

I have consulted for some years to a firm of consultants (about 14 employees) who delineate the "front office"—where secretaries and administrators sit in an open-plan room to do their work— from the separate offices of the "professional staff", the consultants. During a day's workshop set aside for my consultation work, I asked the group to get into pairings of one consultant and one administration person to share with each other the different ways they felt that hierarchy was expressed in the organization. One interesting example was that of a consultant coming into the office and dropping work onto a secretary's desk without any comment. The secretary felt that this was an offensive display of power, yet as the two of them talked it became clear that the consultant felt unable to discuss the work because of the perceived resentment that the secretary had towards the professional staff, and this created a barrier of silence between them. Through these paired "essential conversations", the group could open up their unspoken feelings about hierarchy, which then made it safer to discuss these issues when they arose in the working environment.

Dilemmas and paradoxes

One may well ask, "How do you identify the issues that need to be discussed?" And the best answer I can offer is: "I listen for dilemmas, contradictions, and paradoxes." It is within these constructions that organizations become stuck, and it is also within these constructions that organizations can create new constructions to move forward.

Similar conclusions have been reached by a group of researchers who have studied organizational life through linguistics and the emergence of organizational paradoxes (Czarniawska, 1997). Much of organizational thinking has pursued a coherent, rational theory of how organizations work and, as a result, has consigned the irrational or the paradoxes to the realm of "anomalous communications". But Czarniawska makes the point that "anomalous communication lies at the heart of modern institutions as we know them" (p. 171)

Dilemmas and paradoxes both obstruct and promote change, and, within the social constructionist model I am espousing, it is important that the tension within the paradox and the tendency of paradox to interrupt clear thinking are recognized and tolerated as crucial aspects of renewal. Czarniawska writes:

> To recognise this, it is necessary and sufficient to abandon the idea of planned change as the smooth journey of an idea launched by the leaders. "The resilience to change" presented conventionally as an obstacle and interpreted as psychological backwardness (usually attributed to people at the lower levels of the hierarchy) becomes in political terms, the right to question the ideas that are presented as unavoidable. [p. 172]

I see a difference between dilemmas and paradoxes which have proved helpful to me in my organizational work. A dilemma is easily elicited by asking people what they aspire to and what is restraining them from moving ahead in that direction. I relate dilemmas to "conflicts of action", and I find that clients are usually aware through discussion of their own conflicts. On the other hand, paradoxes are more "conflicts of thinking". They emerge from our own form of logic and use of language, and, since we are trapped by the paradox of trying to untangle our own logical contradictions using our own "flawed" logic, we are trying to do the impossible. So, it is more difficult to grasp such paradoxes.

Several of these points can be illustrated in work I have been doing with a small specialist psychology service. During a half-day consultation with the staff, the group was critical of its manager for not creating a better atmosphere in the service. The individuals wanted an atmosphere in which people could work with their differences and respect each other as professional colleagues. But to change the atmosphere, they would need to take more personal responsibility for the way they spoke and listened to each other, which is not about management from above but about being personally accountable to others for changing the organization. From the manager's point of view, she felt the criticism, but she also felt trapped about how to manage something that seemed to be in the hands of the individuals, and she fluctuated between high levels of managerial activity and periods of cajoling staff to "get on with their work".

This dynamic could be framed as a dilemma, "a conflict of action", in the following way: "I want to work in a service that has a different atmosphere, but I don't know what I can do because I am not responsible for managing the staff relations." The dynamic could also be framed as an organizational paradox or a "conflict of thinking" in the following way: "Let go of management in order to have a better-managed service." We discussed these issues in the group about mid-way through the half-day session.

The consultant must decide how he or she will handle the tension or interruption represented by dilemmas and paradoxes. If they are resolved too quickly, the participants can avoid the fundamental change of thinking required to dissolve or burst the paradox. Paradox paralyzes routine thinking and behaviour. But if the consultant can allow the tension to be tolerated and examined, new ideas will emerge.

And so it was with the half-day meeting. I waited as the minutes ticked by and the end of our consultation approached. Eventually, I asked the individuals what responsibility they wanted to take to change the service, and two ideas emerged. (1) Several staff members agreed to take responsibility for convening a staff meeting for the purpose of discussing how staff could share and respect their differences. (2) Another two staff felt that there should be stronger links between the staff and the manager, and therefore they proposed to work alongside the manager, sharing the attendance at some external meetings and working together to do some strategic planning for the future. This was an example of staying with the paradox until new ideas emerged that addressed the apparent gap in the conflicting sides of the paradox.

Another resolution of organization paradoxes comes from asking people to place the paradox in a narrative context—that is, by introducing an explanatory story and placing events in sequence, paradoxes can be resolved. This is a relatively new endeavour in the organizational field, but readers should refer to Czarniawska (1997) for further discussion of this approach.

Whereas paradoxes refer to the logic embedded in our language, I use the concept of "dilemma" in constructing conversations because it is a handy, easy-to-use concept that broadly defines any situation in which someone is torn between two or more possible actions. It is a "state" of discomfort that usually arises when people become aware of possible conflicting actions facing them as a result of their thoughts and feelings.

I like this concept very much for two reasons: (1) everyone knows what you are talking about or, more importantly, what a dilemma feels like, and they will readily discuss the topic; and (2) it represents a "place" where people are stuck but want to move away from, and this desire to get off the "horns of a dilemma" represents potential motivation for individuals and groups to change.

I try to establish with clients the idea that organizations move forward by having these "essential conversations". I think of the process as "getting the right people together to talk about the right issue". No one will know for sure who are the right people nor what is the right issue, but this is a start. This is a way of thinking about the organization as a socially constructed entity. It exists in the constructs created through dialogue.

I find that when all the participants ask themselves this question and commit themselves to the conversation, they are unerring in identifying the issues that slow their development. There are often unresolved issues from the past—an undercurrent of resentment about inequalities, unspoken rivalries and competition amongst staff, unclear aims and tasks from management—but if I can make the setting safe enough and devolve responsibility to the staff, I find that they will use the essential conversation to build new relationships and structures for the future.

Conversations must not only straddle different points of view, but should take place in a larger context in which dilemmas and paradoxes and differences are valued; personal experiences such as tension, uncertainty, and the interruption of thought should be tolerated as essential ingredients in the process of change.

Action plans

Question: How do you make God laugh?
Answer: Tell Him/Her you've got a plan.

In *Mind and Nature* (1979) Gregory Bateson described a relationship between the *process* that we observe and the *form* into which we put it, which then becomes the basis for observing a different process, which leads to the creation of a new form, and so on. And I find it most helpful to apply this "zigzag ladder" to the relationship between our actions and the meaning we attribute to our actions: we observe an action (action A) and describe it in language and give it meaning, which then leads us to act differently (action B); we, and others, observe action B, describe and give it meaning, which leads to action C; and so on. This is a powerful metaphor that supports the process of change in organizations because they are places of public conversation. Employees learn about their own organization not by what is said or printed in annual reports, but by what they observe others doing. "What do people wear", "How are mistakes to be dealt with?" "How is hierarchy recognized", "How personal can people be?" are all examples of raw data, of what is observed in order to reach a conclusion about the type of organization that they are working in.

When people change their behaviour, this is observed by another, and basic assumptions about the organization can change, or at least be suspended, awaiting further evidence of the change in observed behaviour. Much of the consultation work will be about people's perceptions and subsequent meanings, or what I prefer to call their beliefs about themselves and others, and this is a valuable part of the change process; sooner or later, however, the beliefs must be transformed into action.

Organizational work, such as consultation, offers several timely opportunities for transforming beliefs into action. The first is in consolidating the learning from the consultation itself and presenting immediate changes in how people will act. This model works very well when consultation takes place over a series of meetings and tasks are set at the end of one meeting and then reported back at the next. The second is a long-term process and uses the impetus of the consultation work to build new structures (such as lines of accountability, new tasks, or different meetings) that will maintain essential conversations and relationships over time, and long after the consultant has left the field.

> One example of setting immediate tasks is based on work with a multidisciplinary mental health team (with 14 employees) which took place over four sessions. The initial concern of the team convenor was a lack of team cohesiveness and team identity. Using the systemic concepts of the whole being made up of parts, I presumed from my previous planning meeting with a steering group that the staff were unclear about the sanction and support they were entitled to from their own disciplines to participate in this multidisciplinary team. (This is similar to the "Daisy" model I have described in another book [Campbell, 1995], in which each discipline is seen as one petal contributing to making the whole flower—or the whole multidisciplinary team.)
>
> Towards the end of the session, I asked each discipline group within the team to discuss what they thought they needed to discuss with their "back-home" discipline groups or discipline heads in order for their "back-home" discipline to value the mental health team more strongly. They arrived at the following proposals:
>
> • Social workers: needed to discuss the amount of their time that was appropriate to allocate to the mental health team.
>
> • Occupational therapists: wanted to discuss changing their status to become "community occupational therapists".
>
> • Nurses: needed to speak to their manager to change the system of ward rounds so that they could devote more time to the team.
>
> • Psychologists: were going to produce an audit of both psychologists' work on the team to present to their manager.
>
> In this way, each group related their membership of the team to ongoing issues specific to each "back-home" discipline, and they were all asked to carry out these discussions and report back at the second meeting in one month's time.
>
> At the next meeting, it was clear that the "back-home" discus-

sions had been very fruitful. Generally, they highlighted areas of confusion between membership in the discipline and membership in the team, and several groups established further meetings to clarify their roles and, in the case of the nurses, create a new title for themselves.

This second meeting took a different focus—that is, on the organization of the team itself. Because it covered a large geographical area, the team was divided in two: the North Team and South Team. Although this seemed necessary, it also made the team feel more fragmented. I eventually concluded that it would be helpful to have one "essential conversation" about this dilemma, or, more specifically, a conversation about how they could combine the need to cover a wide geographical area and also reduce the sense of fragmentation. These issues, as discussed earlier, represented boundaries between different structures and functions. This is where dilemmas arise, and this is where the "essential conversations" should take place.

We opened up the possibilities for this conversation by doing several things: We established that there were three areas of activity the team wanted to be engaged in: the functional area of seeing clients, the political area of building a strong profile within the Trust, and the area of professional development, in which team members wanted to get together to share their experiences and discuss cases. Each area of activity could require a different concept of "team" and different structures. We also threw open the possibilities of creating any type of organization through their discussion. We talked about "brain-storming" and not being constrained by the past or by their disciplines. They wanted the opportunity to have a free-wheeling discussion, and to look at the consequences when they reported back in a month's time.

CHAPTER FIVE

Structures for the future

Consultation in the social constructionist approach is not about solving problems once and for all, but about changing the way employees understand the construction of problems in the first place, and the way problems can be deconstructed and re-constructed through conversation. If the employees come to value this process, preparing for the future becomes an exercise in ensuring that essential conversations can take place to develop the necessary strategies and structures for the future.

The social constructionist model suggests that an organization needs opportunities to continue essential conversations long after the consultant has left the field. This is one place where social construction and structure have a reciprocal relationship. They need each other. The conversation creates structures that all can agree on, and these structures ensure that further conversations will be possible to tackle new problems and articulate new organizational values and create new structures.

One structure that clearly possesses the potential to maintain a social constructionist process is the staff meeting. This is one place where the organization is continually being constructed through conversation amongst its members. It is also the place where the more formal constructions such as policies and procedures are hammered out, and the more informal constructions of values and opinions are established.

It can be very helpful, as part of a consultation, to review the different meetings that the staff participate in. I find that if I learn how often people meet, for how long, and with what agenda, I can understand something about what opportunities are available to have essential conversations that bring problems to light and also create new realities for the organization. I am interested, for example, in whether all the meeting times are taken up "doing business" or whether there are opportunities to step back and discuss the question, "How are we doing as an organization?"— that is, whether there are chances to move back and forth on Bateson's ladder between action and reflection.

I am also interested to know how the staff manage their differences and resolve the inevitable conflicts. Unless time is set aside and protected, these are the issues that will be neglected, because they are uncomfortable and always raise the spectre of making working relationships worse than they already are.

As a consultant, I try to take the necessary time at the end of my work to plan for the future, and I would normally discuss the issue of future conversations in the organization. I invite the staff to think about how they will keep the ideas from the consultation work alive and how they will tackle unforeseen problems in the future. I ask: "Who will need to talk to whom? when? and about what?" "Do they have the necessary time for meeting? or do they have some protected space within the existing meetings?"

I have learnt that these conversations do not just happen but need support in several ways:

1. The *meaning* of setting aside time for this purpose should be explored sufficiently so that commitments and competing demands for time can be incorporated into the plans for future meetings. This is particularly important if such meetings represent a change in the culture which inevitably challenges old ways.

2. The *structures* of where and when and with whom the meetings will take place should be discussed and agreed by staff.

3. The *accountability* of these meetings should also be agreed. It may be helpful for one person, or a small group, to carry responsibility on behalf of the organization for the meetings. There will be questions of preserving the space, dealing with non-attenders, and circulating feedback from the conversations. Monitoring the progress of these meetings over time is important because adjustments will be necessary as the priorities of the organization change. I find that if there is one "champion" or group looking after these meetings, they will protect the space as pressures increase to use the meetings in other ways. For example, what is referred to as "pressure of work" will intrude so that staff will fill the space with "more important tasks" and not attend meetings, or the agenda may be hijacked away from conversations about how the organization is getting on towards clarifying operational procedures.

I am not advocating that organizations become "navel-gazing" and self-reflective at the expense of getting on with the job; there should always be a balance between the action and reflection, as discussed earlier. I am making a different point: that we decide how to "act" and how to "be" in our organization as the result of conversations, whether these are about the values of dealing with clients or the washing-up rota. Attention must be paid to the way realities are created through conversations, and space must be provided to have new conversations to address the inevitable tensions that arise between "the way we used to do things" and "the way we want to do them in the future."

Finally, I have found that it may also be helpful if I include myself in the accountability process, by asking the organization to keep me informed about the progress of their plans. I have also at times negotiated to do a follow-up visit (or, at the least, to telephone) to review their progress. This keeps me in the picture and enables the staff to feel some accountability to me and to the previous work we have done together.

On several occasions, I have left an evaluation form with the staff group to fill in and return to me. I usually "tailor" the questionnaire to fit the agency and the work we have done, both to give the staff the opportunity to clarify what they have taken from the work and to give me feedback about specific issues that

---

Evaluation Form

(This is an entirely optional invitation to provide some feedback about the recent team consultations. The information will be helpful to me, but you may also appreciate the chance the "step back" and comment.)

— In relation to our team consultation meetings, would you have preferred to have them structured in a different way?

— Are there certain themes that should have been discussed further? Or others that were discussed too much?

— Do you have any clearer ideas of what *you* can do if you want to improve the team atmosphere in the team?

— Do you have any clearer idea of what *others* can do if they want to improve the team atmosphere?

— Any general comments?

FIGURE 1

emerged. A recent questionnaire that I produced following four meetings with a mental health team over four months is presented in Figure 1.

> One example of a "future structure" resulted from my work with a multidisciplinary team (of 10 employees) responsible for providing services to learning-disabled clients. One issue that emerged in our work was that the staff felt that they could not discuss the personal stresses that the work created for all of them. They seemed to be rushed off their feet with work, and, when they did meet, time was taken to discuss cases and establish

procedures. They wanted a different space in which to share and get support for more personal responses to the work.

We all worked to design a new meeting for this purpose. In order that the meeting was not overtaken by agency or client issues, we gave the meeting a name, "The Reflective Meeting", and ground rules. It was to be held on Mondays and to be convened by one staff member for a month, then passed to the next, on a rota basis. The main ground rules were that people were free to share whatever they wanted to share, with the aim "to help others to understand personal issues that have a bearing on my work in the team". They agreed that they might want to share something recent from their previous weekend or something of a more enduring nature about their reactions to clients, or they might also choose to say nothing on a particular Monday. The second ground rule, which has proved crucial, is that no further discussion of the issues takes place outside the reflective meeting and no decisions about the working of the agency can be taken on the basis of the discussion in the reflective meeting. Instead, if anyone thinks that some changes should be made in the agency, it was agreed that this would be raised in the regular business meeting—a different context.

The feedback from this structured meeting has been very good. I know that many agencies—particularly those who have to manage the stress of therapeutic relationships—use similar reflective groups. In this case, it proved important to have full staff agreement for such a meeting and to carve out a protected space in the weekly timetable.

PART III

CASE ILLUSTRATIONS

CHAPTER SIX

Conversations and beliefs

I have worked as a consultant to a small marital mediation service (10 staff) on and off for several years. They asked me to spend one and a half days with them following a difficult year in which several staff had had personal problems that took their attention away from work and left the agency feeling the need to pull together and clarify its direction.

Because of the personal preoccupations of the staff, I thought they might like to begin by each person telling the group "where they were" as individuals working in this agency. I invited them to say what they wanted the group to understand about what was on their minds about themselves and their work. During this round, a number of people spoke of a dwindling creativity in the work. I simply noted this to myself.

I often begin working in this way. It connects me with the experience of individuals in the group, but it is also the beginning of a social construction process, because each staff member can listen attentively to the others.

For the second discussion, I asked what issues needed to be addressed to enable the agency to change in ways they each wanted. One person said that they needed to talk about leadership, another said that the structures and procedures in the agency make them anxious about making mistakes and restrict their creativity, while a third referred to the staff being too tolerant of each other and lowering the standards they expected from their work.

Next, I tried to pull these themes together into one overarching theme, or topic, for an "essential conversation", which would open these topics up and give the staff a chance to see these issues differently. I asked them to discuss, in groups of three, the kinds of structures that they felt would enhance rather than stifle creativity, and together they produced a list of twelve "structures" that they wanted to put into place, from appointment books and more precise minute-taking, to organizing themselves into project teams and setting up awaydays for staff. While all of these are laudable and important to implement, the agency was now face to face with the question of how they would overcome the organization's reluctance to change. In fact, one of the participants said, "We have been here before", implying that they had already been that far but had gone no further in the process of change.

I would conceptualize this as my struggle to identify the right level for the essential conversation. In other words, we may have settled for a conversation that addressed dilemmas that were of lesser importance relative to the larger, more encompassing dilemmas facing the organization. If a consultant is clever enough to realize the right level at the first try, he or she should continue to question the group about the nature of the dilemma until it "expands", or seems encompassing enough, to stimulate a new construction of the organization, rather than, as in this case, taking the organization towards a constructive conversation where they had "already been". But if the consultant does not know at what level to conceptualize the presenting dilemma in order to lead to more comprehensive, "second-order" change, the only option is to wait, to keep talking, and to listen very carefully to what people say.

My style is to follow the process of the group and to rely on them to provide new ideas that will allow us all to make hypotheses about the most pertinent dilemma that needs discussing. I therefore asked the group about the problem of "having been here before" and what they felt were the biggest obstacles preventing the agency moving beyond this stage. The staff identified a process whereby they all publicly claimed to be different and valued their differences, but whenever the differences led to conflict, this was defused by retreating from the differences and claiming personal responsibility for the disagreement: "It must have something to do with me", as one of them put it.

This is an example of an agency socially constructing, through their action and beliefs, ideas about conflict and how it should be managed. Certain ideas are available within the discourse of this agency (and others are not). One might say that this discourse is helpful in letting people get on with their work, but it may offer limited possibilities for new ideas when work is not going smoothly, as in the case of this agency.

But as staff members are getting on with their work, they are embedded in this discourse and are unlikely to step back and observe how their discourse about conflict is limiting their ability to tackle a new situation. By organizing conversations such as these, staff members are given the opportunity to create new constructs or widen the discourse about conflict. It is crucial that all of the staff participate in this process, so that the new discourse represents all of the individual views in the agency. If this does not happen, I have found that remnants from the old discourse get in the way and block the forward progress of the agency.

This led me to consider an exercise in which they could experience talking about their differences and, in the safety of a facilitated consultation, break through the barrier that had held them back in the past.

Exercise 3: Exploring differences

I asked the staff to return to their groups of three and for a pair in each group to explore the following question: "When you observe or think about your partner, what are the major differences between you? See if you can learn something about why this difference is important to your partner and how it is linked to their creativity." Since this was a new experience for the staff, I asked the third person in each group to be an observer and "security guard" to ensure that people felt that they were taking some risks within a safe atmosphere and were at liberty to halt the process at any stage.

The reason I asked the group to do this exercise was that I wanted to provide an opportunity for the staff to be able to talk about conflict. In this case, since they had not talked about it openly, it seemed best to break it down into manageable, relatively safe conversations about difference. Difference lies at the heart of conflict, and it is sometimes easier for a group to face larger conflicts that grip the entire agency if they first have the experience of managing a smaller "potential conflict" in the form of differences between two individuals.

It does not sound particularly risky when reading this account on paper; however, this and similar exercises about differences must be constructed with a clear view of the agency and the anxieties that may be raised. For this agency, it seemed like a significant step forward; one member did not initially want to take part, but after some discussion he agreed and the entire staff took part. They said later that it was made easier with the addition of the "security guard" and the outside facilitator.

From this experience, which placed each participant in a dyadic relationship of differences, I wanted to broaden the scope so that these people would also begin to see themselves contributing to the creation and maintenance of the agency's belief system or discourse about difference and change. I have found that people feel more confident dealing with their colleagues after they have had a face-to-face discussion of differences, but they begin to see their organization differently once they have stepped back to see how they contribute to the creation of the organization's belief system or the socially constructed organization.

To nudge the group in this direction and to complement the previous exercise, I began to discuss my ideas about how they have learned two things: (1) what kind of organization they are, and (2) how they should and should not behave. (These ideas are discussed in more detail in chapter 3.) I stressed the idea that they could only develop their belief about how to be by observing and attributing meaning to the behaviour of their colleagues, and that this was a dynamic process of learning by seeing the beliefs enacted as well as seeing the beliefs not being enacted. À la Derrida, I talked about the absence of good behaviour helping them understand which good behaviour was required in their agency, and

that they all took part in this social construction by what they did
or did not do and by what they observed others doing and not
doing.

I then walked up to the flipchart and wrote on it one of their
guiding beliefs that had emerged during the day:

> "We are an organization that is a good place to work in, we are
> successful, and we have learned that it is better not to have too
> many great differences amongst us."

When we reviewed the history of the agency, it was clear that this
guiding belief had been very helpful in lifting them out of an
earlier stressful period in which staff were not speaking to one
another. However, at present the prohibition about differences
was stifling creativity and further development, and they were
keen to discuss this.

I asked them to discuss, again in groups of three, what they did
that contributed to the creation of this guiding belief. There was
puzzlement, so I added: "The only way you have learned how
your agency is supposed to be is by observing and listening to each
other over the years. So what do you think you have you done, or
not done, that others have observed and used as data to decide
'this is the kind of organization we are' or 'this is the correct belief
for us'?' They then got busy with their discussions.

During the feedback to the whole group I asked them what was
interesting or what they had learnt from the discussion, and one
of them, the administrator, said, "I can see that being too kind in
the office and not having high expectations is the opposite of what
we are trying to do". Another staff member said that she realized
that she held back from agreeing too much with colleagues about
changes because she could become too powerful and then rock the
boat of the comfortable agency.

The final piece of work in this consultation focused on the
relationship between leader and staff. Various comments made
during the two days of this work alerted me to this relationship as
an important issue for further developments of the agency, and I
initiated this conversation myself. This is an example of tension at
the interface between two parts of the whole: the director of the

service and the staff group. Many problems arise when two sub-groups lose sight of their connectedness and begin to see their problems as the responsibility of "the other". Conversations at this interface are a powerful means of reestablishing the sense of connectedness.

During the lunch break I had asked the director how he felt about this, and he was agreeable to sitting in front of the group and taking part in an "interactional" (i.e. back-and-forth) discussion with his staff. I prefaced the discussion by referring to the systemic principles that suggest that the quality of leadership is influenced by the behaviour of the "followers" just as their behaviour is affected by the leader, and both parties have it within their power to change the nature of this relationship (see chapter 1).

The director spoke first, saying that he felt that the staff were "being too careful with me". He had recently been preoccupied by a family illness and wondered if the staff consequently saw him as vulnerable. One of the staff replied, saying that it was difficult for her to know how to respond to the director when he says things like, "I have let you down", because it is too personal. Others said that this had been the director's style of leadership long before the family difficulties. Other comments indicated that the director was personally involved in many day-to-day decisions, a situation they all wanted to change. This seemed like a good moment to ask what the staff did that encouraged this behaviour in the director, and they gave recognizable examples. The complementary question is, what did he do that made it difficult for them to change their behaviour and thus the relationship between them? The discussion closed with an acknowledgement that all parties would try to shift the agency from a culture of personal decision-making towards one that had more policies and roles to aid decision-making. This in turn led to a working party that would clarify policy for several areas of ambiguity. This was a discussion that needed to continue after my departure, and I suggested that they allocate some time during staff meetings to do so.

This case example highlights several ways in which social constructionist thinking can be applied to work with organizations. The first is the use of different types of conversations to socially construct new ideas about differences and conflict in the agency.

Conversations can be built up from "safer" dyadic conversations to larger discussions amongst the whole staff. The second is the understanding that beliefs about differences and conflict are socially constructed from observations and conversations in the past. These no longer seemed appropriate for this agency today, and changing the beliefs was a matter of the staff talking differently about conflict and then observing themselves behaving differently.

CHAPTER SEVEN

Learning the hard way

I think there is much to be gained from looking at cases that did not seem to go so well. They provide a rich opportunity for learning about—and from—ways that, in the words of the balloonist, "didn't fail, . . . just didn't work". It is in this spirit that I present the following case

I was asked to work with a small organization that provided housing and support services for a wide range of clients. The organization consisted of two departmental managers (both men), the director (a woman), and about 50 employees. The director approached me about the work saying that she would interview several prospective consultants, including myself, and then choose the best person for the job. She also asked permission to contact two previous clients of mine to assess the outcome of my work. This seemed eminently appropriate, but there was something about the way the director approached this that put me on the defensive, and I remember feeling more pressure than usual to show myself as competent and successful.

The relevant background is that the director had been a fairly recent outside appointment, chosen over one of the managers who had applied as an internal applicant for the director's position. There was bad feeling between them. The director said that she wanted to help to improve the relationship between her and the manager. She felt that the manager was not good enough at his own job but would not take any advice from her because of the unresolved rivalry and disappointment about not getting the post of director. The manager, on the other hand, felt that the management of his department was being undermined by the director, as his own staff would frequently go behind his back to make a complaint and the director allowed this to happen. The director used these incidents to support her view that the manager did not communicate well enough with his own staff. A final factor is that the Board tended to split down the middle, half supporting the director, the other half believing that the manager was talented and dynamic and should stay on regardless of any lapses in his management style. The third member of this executive, the other manager, tended to take a noncommittal position between the two protagonists.

One can see from the way this case was presented that the problem, as defined by the director, was socially constructed out of many different conversations and actions that had taken place among different members of the system: the director and the manager, the manager and his staff, and the director and the Board. My dilemma was to know which kind of conversation, and amongst whom, would lead to the most rapid but also most lasting change in the way the relationship between the director and manager was seen.

Another dilemma facing me was how to deal with the issue of power and hierarchy. Would the director and the manager be free enough to allow their ideas to be influenced by a conversation with the other, or was the hierarchical, managerial relationship so powerful that this would be impossible? This question is important to ask because it helps a consultant decide what should be addressed in the discussions amongst staff.

I was aware of many different ideas, each one leading to a different course of action:

- I could say that this manager did not have the necessary skill to be able to manage a staff group in these circumstances. By putting the emphasis on this part of the process, I would be using a learning model of organizational process and might consider teaching the manager some new skills and working directly with him and his staff.

- I might also say that the director and the manager are locked into a relationship that is heavily influenced by their characters and backgrounds. This psychological model suggests that individual sessions to explore their feelings about authority, control, and rivalry might be helpful in breaking the deadlock.

- Or I could say that the relationship between the director and the manager was socially constructed by the *organization as a whole* through the behaviour, and conversation, of the executives, the staff, and the Board. This would connect to the social constructionist model and lead to setting up various "essential conversations" amongst these people about how the organization should be managed and what kinds of relationships were necessary to support the process.

Since each of these hypotheses can contribute something to the larger picture of what is going on, I chose to combine my thoughts with the following proposal: I thought it would help to begin with individual interviews with each of the three executives in order to create a safe environment. I could hear their story, connect with them personally, and begin to explore what the meaning of the conflictual relationship was for each of them. I would follow this by holding a meeting with the three of them, and at that meeting I would make a proposal for the future. I was also thinking that it might be helpful at a later stage to work with the manager and his staff group; however, this had to be done carefully, because if broached too early it would place me on the side of the director, who was critical of the manager.

Interestingly, during the individual interviews many gender issues arose. The director, who was probing her own experience to figure out what was going on, spoke about a difficult relationship with her father and speculated about whether this exacerbated the conflict with the manager; for his part, the manager, who was much less inclined to self-exploration, spoke of his powerful mother. When we all met together, the emerging theme was organizational. The director said: "I am in charge here and I have to get results or my head is on the block, so you [the manager] have got to perform better." The manager replied: "I can't improve my relations with my staff with you undermining my authority and continually looking over my shoulder." Meanwhile, the other manager was truly caught in the crossfire between these two. My sense during this meeting was that the "essential conversation" was about how they could trust each other enough to feel that they could work together as one team, rather than as "two opponents and an onlooker." And this became the theme for the remaining discussion.

We agreed to have several more similar meetings at monthly intervals, and during the second visit I spent more time with the joint management team. I felt that the increasing participation of the "onlooker" manager was helpful in creating more of a team atmosphere amongst them; however, during the meeting this manager told me (the others already knew) that he and his family were emigrating in a few months.

I was concerned about what would happen in the management team before our next meeting, as I was not confident that the group could restrain themselves from arguments and blame, which could escalate without the presence of a facilitator. In addition to any understanding of their relationships gleaned in our meeting, I decided to make two interventions that would also support them through structured conversations.

The first suggestion was that they should set aside time in each of their executive meetings to discuss ways in which they as a group could promote the development of the entire staff and that they should prepare a short written statement about how they would do this. My intention in proposing this was to reinforce them as a team with shared responsibilities for the staff, and to build a sense of a future together to shift them from their preoccupation with the past.

The second suggestion was that they should agree to stick to their agenda during their meeting but allow themselves ten minutes at the end of each meeting to discuss how they felt they had got on as a group during the meeting—for example, whether any-one felt that he or she was not respected or listened to or could not make his or her views clear to the others. The purpose of this suggestion was to acknowledge the need for an ongoing dialogue about their relationships, particularly the mutual blame between the director and the manager, and to set aside a protected space to reflect upon this, so that the arguing did not spill over into other working conversations.

I came back a month later to find that the director and the manager had had a big row, and the latter had submitted his resignation, only to retract it after conciliatory gestures from the director. They had tried to carry out the tasks that I set them, but the acrimony flared up to undermine the process each time. During my meeting with the three executives, I noticed that the manager who was emigrating was also less engaged with the process of this meeting, as though she had mentally "moved on". However, I felt an easing of the tension between the other two. For the first time I felt that they could sympathetically understand the position of the other, and much of this meeting was spent going back and forth between them, giving each one the chance to listen to and then clarify the other's impression of them. Towards the end, I made the next monthly appointment and recommended that they continue using their meetings as we had previously agreed.

That was the last time I saw them. About a week before my next visit, the director telephoned to tell me that there had been more rows and that the manager had resigned a few days earlier. The manager would be busy winding down his work with the staff in his department and did not want to take the time for our monthly meeting. The director, likewise, said that she wanted to postpone our meeting for a few weeks to take stock of the changes that were going on.

* * *

So what *was* going on? In spite of the brevity of this resumé, I hope the reader will speculate with me about what happened and what lesson might be carried away from this work. The questions I ask myself are: "How do we evaluate our own work?" or "What constitutes a success or a failure?" This certainly felt like a failure to me, because my efforts to improve the relationships sufficiently for them to continue working together were not successful, and the manager left the organization. This leads to the further question of whether I *should* evaluate this work on the basis of whether the manager continued in the organization or decided to leave. It could be argued that the situation was intractable and that therefore the consultation may in fact have been helpful by focusing on the difficulties in the relationship, bringing issues to a head, and enabling the manager to make the "healthy" decision to leave rather than to struggle on in a bad working environment.

More specific questions are also raised by this case, such as: "Could I have done things differently in my work with the relationship between director and manager?" I think I was affected more than I realized at the time by the way the director vetted me for the job. Upon reflection, I am now aware that I felt more pressure to measure up to the director's high standards, and in this case the standards seemed to translate into the injunction: "Make the manager into a more effective manager." If I had been hired by the director and had accepted this injunction, I might have been seen by the manager as biased and therefore a person who would be difficult to trust and work with. Although I considered this carefully at the beginning of the work, I did not have this open conversation in the presence of the three members of the management team; perhaps I should have.

I am also aware that I accepted a contract to work with the organization at monthly intervals, which suited their wishes in terms of workload and budget constraints. With hindsight, perhaps I should have worked more intensively with the three executives and not left such long gaps for mutual blame to escalate between sessions.

There is also the question of the prioritization of my original hypothesis about this case. Instead of postponing any work with the manager and her staff until a later stage, perhaps I could have done this work simultaneously with the work with the management team. There was the inevitable risk of accepting the director's opinion that the manager was the problem, but improved working relations with his staff might also have given the manager more confidence about his ability to manage and more confidence about being managed from above by the director.

One lesson I hope I have learnt from this experience is that of maintaining the right to change the working contract on the basis of what seems right for a particular problem, rather than what was agreed in a prior contract.

Final thoughts

This book has tried to place social constructionism in the market-place alongside previous books that describe organizations from a systemic perspective (e.g. Campbell et al., 1994). I see social constructionism as a separate field which nevertheless incorporates many concepts that are also articulated in the systemic framework, such as feedback, recursiveness, meaning systems, and seeing a "whole made up of parts". Social constructionism emphasizes different concepts such as social discourse, joint action, and dialogic communication. While this book has put a boundary around social constructionism, it remains only a part of the process that makes organizations what they are. The other part is the structures and resources that limit what an organization can do.

By this, I mean that as organizations interact with employees and the outside world, they socially construct their view of how the organization should be; they then use these constructions to build structures and policies, which, in turn, affect what it is possible to construct in the next phase of the social construction process. And this continues ad infinitum. It seems to me that this reciprocal process is paramount. Changing government legislation or employment practices will affect the social construction of the organization as surely as the social construction process leads to new structures.

As I reach the end of this book, I find myself in a critical frame of mind. Does the book really demonstrate that social constructionist ideas are significantly different to stand alone as a theoretical model for work with organizations? And perhaps at this stage the answer should be: "not yet". I bristle at the tendency of many of us practitioners to wrap explanations around our work prematurely, thus creating the dominant discourse and inhibiting alternative explanations, yet some attempt at conceptualizing is necessary in order to create a language to communicate to the reader. I am aware that there is further to go before I would feel confident to describe my work as consistently following a model. My own thinking is an amalgam of both systemic and social constructionist ideas, and somehow these have co-mingled, along with all the myriad influences in my life, to produce the framework described in this book. I have found that social constructionism helps me explain some of the things I have been doing for many years, such as arranging structured conversations, but it has also inspired me to try new ways of seeing organization activity, such as how the organization offers its members only certain constructs with which to negotiate their realities. When I ask the question, "Do social constructionist ideas really make any difference to the way I actually work with organizations?", I am inclined to reply: "They are beginning to."

Finally, I am reminded of the quote by Harold Bloom (Rorty, 1989) that the meaning of the book is simply that there "have been" other similar books, and that this book may lend some meaning to books, or models of consultation, that lie in the future.

REFERENCES AND BIBLIOGRAPHY

Anderson, H., & Goolishian, H. (1988). Human systems as linguistic systems: evolving ideas about the implications for theory and practice. *Family Process*, 27: 371–93.

Anderson, H., & Goolishian, H. (1992). The client is the expert: a not-knowing approach to therapy. In: S. McNamee & K. Gergen (Eds), *Therapy as Social Construction*. London: Sage.

Anderson, H., Goolishian, H., & Winderman, L. (1986). Problem-determined systems: towards transformation in family therapy. *Journal of Strategic and Systemic Therapies*, 5: 1–13.

Ashby, R. (1956). *Introduction to Cybernetics*. New York: Chapman and Hall.

Austin, J. L. (1962). *How to Do Things with Words*. Oxford: Oxford University Press.

Bakhtin, M. M. (1981). *The Dialogic Imagination*. Austin, TX: University of Texas Press.

Bakhtin, M. M. (1986). *Speech Genres and Other Late Essays*, ed. C. Emerson & M. Holquist, trans. V. W. McGee. Austin, TX: University of Texas Press.

Bakhtin, M. M. (1993). *Toward a Philosophy of the Act*, ed. M. Holquist, trans. and notes V. Lianpov. Austin, TX: University of Texas Press.

Bateson, G. (1972). *Steps to an Ecology of Mind.* New York: Ballantine.

Bateson, G. (1979). *Mind and Nature.* New York: Dutton.

Becker, C., Chasin, L., Chasin, R., Herzig, M., & Roth, S. (1995). From stuck debate to new conversation on controversial issues: a report from the Public Conversations Project. *Journal of Feminist Family Therapy, 7* (1–2): 143–163.

Bender, C. (1998). Bakhtinian perspectives on "everyday life" sociology. In: *Bakhtin and the Human Sciences* (pp. 181–195), ed. M. Bell & M. Gardiner. London: Sage.

Benhabib, S. (1990). Afterword: communicative ethics and current controversies in practical philosophy. In: S. Benhabib & F. Dallmayr, *The Communicative Ethics Controversy.* Cambridge, MA: MIT Press.

Benveniste, E. (1971). *Problems in General Linguistics.* Miami, FL: University of Miami Press.

Berger, P., & Luckmann, T. (1966). *The Social Construction of Reality.* Garden City, NY: Doubleday.

Billig, M. (1990). Rhetoric of social psychology. In: I. Parker & J. Shotter (Eds.), *Deconstructing Social Psychology.* London: Routledge.

Billig, M. (1996). *Arguing and Thinking: Rhetorical Approach to Social Psychology.* Cambridge: Cambridge University Press.

Bion, W. R. (1959). *Experiences in Groups and Other Papers.* New York: Basic Books.

Boscolo, L., Cecchin, G., Hoffman, L., & Penn, P. (1986). *Milan Systemic Family Therapy,* New York: Basic Books.

Burman, E. (1994). *Deconstructing Developmental Psychology.* London: Routledge.

Burr, V. (1995). *An Introduction to Social Constructionism.* London: Routledge.

Campbell, D. (1995). *Learning Consultation: A Systemic Framework.* London: Karnac Books.

Campbell, D. (1996). Connecting personal experience to the primary task: a model for consulting to organisations. *Human Systems, 7* (2–3): 117–130.

Campbell, D., Draper, R., & Huffington, C. (1991). *A Systemic Approach to Consultation.* London: Karnac Books.

Campbell, D., Coldicott, T., & Kinsella, K. (1994). *Systemic Work with Organizations.* London: Karnac Books.

Cecchin, G. (1987). Hypothesizing, circularity and neutrality revisited: an invitation to curiosity. *Family Process, 26:* 405–413.

Changing Organisations: Clinicians as Agents of Change. (1996). *Human Systems* (Special Issue), 7 (2–3).

Cooperrider, D., & Srivastra, S. (1987). Appreciative inquiry in organisational life. *Research in Organisational Change and Development, 1*: 129–169.

Czarniawska, B. (1997). *Narrating the Organization.* Chicago, IL: University of Chicago Press.

Davidson, D. (1984). *Inquiries into Truth and Interpretation.* Oxford: Oxford University Press.

de Peuter, J. (1998). The dialogue of narrative. In: M. Bell & M. Gardiner (Eds.), *Bakhtin and the Human Sciences* (pp. 30–48). London: Sage.

Deetz, S., & White, W. (1999). Relational responsibility or dialogic ethics. In: S. McNamee & K. Bergen (Eds.), *Relational Responsibility* (pp. 111–120). London: Sage.

Derrida, J. (1978). *Writing and Difference.* Chicago, IL: University of Chicago Press.

Drucker, P. (1990). *Managing the Non-Profit Organisation.* Oxford: Butterworth-Heinemann.

Edwards, D., & Potter, J. (1992). *Discursive Psychology.* London: Sage.

Foucault, M. (1972). *The Archaeology of Knowledge,* trans, A. M. Sheridan. London: Tavistock Publications.

Foucault, M. (1980). Power and strategies. In: *Power/Knowledge: Selected Interviews and Other Writings* 1972–1977, ed. C. Gordon. New York: Pantheon Books.

Geertz, C. (1973). *The Interpretation of Cultures.* New York: Basic Books.

Geertz, C. (1975). On the nature of anthropological understanding. *American Scientist, 63*: 47–53.

Geertz, C. (1979). From the native's point of view. On the nature of anthropological understanding. In: P. Rabinow & W. Sullivan (Eds.), *Interpretative Social Science.* Berkeley, CA: University of California Press.

Geertz, C. (1983). *Local Knowledge: Further Essays in Interpretative Anthropology.* New York: Basic Books.

Gergen, K. J. (1985). The social constructionist movement in modern psychology. *American Psychologist, 40*: 266–275.

Gergen, K. J. (1989). Warranting voice and the elaboration of the self. In: J. Shotter & K. J. Gergen (Eds.), *Text of Identity.* London: Sage.

Gergen, K. J. (1990). Organisational theory in the postmodern era. In:

M. Reed & M. Hughes (Eds.), *Rethinking Organisation*. London: Sage Publications.

Gergen, K. J. (1994). *Realities and Relationships: Soundings in Social Construction*. Cambridge, MA: Harvard University Press.

Gergen, K. J. (1999). *An Invitation to Social Construction*. London: Sage.

Gergen, M. (1999). Relational responsibility: deconstructive possibilities. In: S. McNamee & K. Gergen, *Relational Responsibility*. Thousand Oaks, CA: Sage.

Guba, E. G., & Lincoln, Y. S. (1989). *Fourth Generation Evaluation*. Newbury, CA: Sage.

Hampden-Turner, C. (1990). *Charting the Corporate Mind*. Oxford: Blackwell.

Harré, R. (1979). *Social Being*. Oxford: Blackwell.

Harré, R. (1986a). An outline of the social constructionist viewpoint. In: R. Harré (Ed.), *The Social Construction of Emotions*. Oxford: Blackwell.

Harré, R. (Ed.) (1986b). *The Social Construction of Emotions*. Oxford: Blackwell.

Harré, R. (1994). *Discursive Psychology*. London: Sage.

Haslebo, G., & Nielsen, K. S. (2000). *Systems and Meaning: Consulting in Organizations*. London: Karnac Books.

Hermans, H., & Kempen, H. (1993). *The Dialogical Self: Meaning as Movement*. San Diego, CA: Academic Press.

Hoffman, L. (1981). *Foundations of Family Therapy*. New York: Basic Books.

Hoffman, L. (1993). *Exchanging Voices*. London: Karnac Books.

Katz, A., & Shotter, J. (1996). Hearing the patient's voice: toward a "social poetics" in diagnostic interviews. *Social Science and Medicine, 43*: 919–931.

Keeney, B. (1983). *Aesthetics of Change*. New York: Guilford Press.

Kitzinger, C., & Wilkinson, S. (1996). Theorising representing the other. In: S. Wilkinson & C. Kitzinger (Eds.), *Representing the Other: A Feminism and Psychology Reader*. London: Sage.

Lakoff, G., & Johnson, M. (1980). *Metaphors We Live By*. Chicago, IL: University of Chicago Press.

Latour, B. (1993). *We Have Never Been Modern*. Hemel Hempstead: Harvester Wheatsheaf.

Mason, B. (1993). Towards positions of safe uncertainty. *Human Systems, 4*: 189–200.

McCaughan, N., & Palmer, B. (1994). *Systems Thinking for Harassed Managers*. London: Karnac Books.

Mead, G. H. (1934a). *Mind, Self and Society*. Chicago, IL: University of Chicago Press.

Mead, G. H. (1934b). *The Social Psychology of George Herbert Mead*. Chicago, IL: University of Chicago Press.

Menzies, I. (1970). *The Functioning of Social Systems as a Defence Against Anxiety*. Tavistock Pamphlet No. 3. London: Tavistock Institute of Human Relations.

Menzies Lyth, I. (1988). *Containing Anxiety in Institutions*. London: Free Association Books.

Miller, E. (1976). *Task and Organisation*. London: Wiley.

Mills, C. W. (1940). Situated actions and vocabularies of motive. *American Sociological Review, 5*: 904–913.

Morgan, G. (1986). *Images of Organisations*. London: Sage.

Phoenix, A., Woollett, A., & Lloyd, E. (Eds.) (1991). *Motherhood: Meanings, Practices and Ideologies*. London: Sage.

Potter, J., & Wetherell, M. (1987). *Discourse and Social Psychology: Beyond Attitudes and Behaviour*. London: Sage.

Rorty, R. (1980). *Philosophy and the Mirror of Nature*. Oxford: Blackwell.

Rorty, R. (1989). *Contingency, Irony & Solidarity*. Cambridge: Cambridge University Press.

Rorty, R. (1991). Inquiry as recontextualization: an anti-dualist account of interpretation. In: *Objectivity, Relativism and Truth* (pp. 93–110). Philosophical Papers 1. New York: Cambridge University Press.

Roth, S. (1999). The uncertain path to dialogue: a meditation. In S. McNamee & K. Gergen (Eds.), *Relational Responsibility* (pp. 93–97). London: Sage.

Said, E. (1994). *Culture and Imperialism*. London: Vintage.

Sampson, E. (1993). *Celebrating the Other*. London: Harvester–Wheatsheaf.

Saussure, F. de (1974). *Course in General Linguistics*. London: Fontana.

Schein, E. (1969). *Process Consultation, Vol. 2*. Reading, MA: Addison-Wesley.

Selvini Palazzoli, M. (1986). *The Hidden Games of Organizations*. Pantheon: New York.

Senge, P. M. (1990). *The Fifth Discipline*. New York: Doubleday.

Shotter, J. (1980). Action, joint action, and intentionality. In: M. Brenner (Ed.), *The Structure of Action*. Oxford: Blackwell.

Shotter, J. (1984). *Social Accountability and Selfhood*. Oxford: Blackwell.

Shotter, J. (1989). Social accountability and the social construction of "you". In: J. Shotter & K. Gergen (Eds.), *Texts of Identity*. London: Sage.

Shotter, J. (1990). Rom Harré: realism and the turn to social constructionism. In: R. Bhaskar & R. Harré (Eds.), *Realism and Human Being*. Oxford: Blackwell.

Shotter, J. (1991). Rhetoric and the social construction of cognitivism. *Theory & Psychology*, 1: 495–513.

Shotter, J. (1992). Bakhtin and Billig: monological versus dialogical practices. *American Behavioural Scientist*, 36: 8–21.

Shotter, J. (1993). *Conversational Realities, Constructing Life through Language*. London: Sage.

Shotter, J., & Billig, M. (1998). A Bakhtinian psychology: from out of the heads of individuals and into the dialogues between them. In: M. Bell & M. Gardiner (Eds.), *Bakhtin and the Human Sciences* (pp. 13–29). London: Sage.

Shotter, J., & Gergen, K. J. (Eds.) (1989). *Texts of Identity*. London: Sage.

Steiner, G. (1989). *Real Presences*. Chicago, IL: University of Chicago Press.

Voloshinov, V. N. (1929). *Marxism and the Philosophy of Language*. Cambridge, MA: Harvard University Press, 1986.

von Bertalanffy, L. (1950). An outline of general systems theory. *British Journal of Philosophical Science*, 1: 134–165.

Von Foerster, H. (1981). *Observing Systems*. Seaside, CA: Intersystems Publications.

White, M. (1991). *Deconstruction and Therapy*. Adelaide: Dulwich Centre Newsletter No. 3.

White, M. (1995). *Re-Authoring Lives*. Adelaide: Dulwich Press.

Willi, J., Frei, R., & Limacher, B. (1993). Couples therapy using the technique of construct differentiation. *Family Process*, 32: 311–321.

Wittgenstein, L. (1953). *Philosophical Investigations*. Oxford: Blackwell.

Wittgenstein, L. (1969). *On Certainty*. Oxford: Blackwell.

Wynne, L., McDaniel, S., & Weber, T. (Eds.) (1986). *Systems Consultation: A New Perspective for Family Therapy*. London: Guilford Press.

INDEX